Like a Tree Planted 11/21/01

A "Connections" Book

Like a Tree Planted

An Exploration of Psalms and Parables Through Metaphor

Barbara Green, O.P.

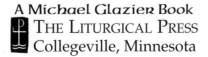

A Michael Glazier Book
THE LITURGICAL PRESS
Collegeville, Minnesota

Cover design by Ann Blattner. Watercolor by Ethel Boyle.

A Michael Glazier Book published by The Liturgical Press.

The English translation of Psalms 1, 7, 8, 18, 23, 27, 35, and 41 from the *Liturgical Psalter* © 1994, International Committee on English in the Liturgy, Inc. All rights reserved.

2	3	4	5	6	7	8

Library of Congress Cataloging-in-Publication Data

Green, Barbara, 1946–
    Like a tree planted : an exploration of psalms and parables through metaphor / Barbara Green.
        p.   cm.
    "A Michael Glazier book."
    Includes bibliographical references.
    ISBN 0-8146-5869-5
    1. Bible. O.T. Psalms—Criticism, interpretation, etc. 2. Bible. N.T. Luke— Criticism, interpretation, etc. 3. Jesus Christ—Parables. 4. Trees in the Bible. 5. Metaphor in the Bible. I. Title.
BS1430.2.G74   1997
223'.2066—dc21   97-2323
                                                                          CIP

To Marcella, in appreciation of
a wonderful friendship.

Acknowledgments

Like A Tree Planted grew, like a tree, from many wonderful conversations and insights generated in workshops and retreats. I am particularly grateful to Brendan McAnerney's Seminarium in Blessed Sacrament Parish, Seattle, Washington; to the Cistercian Men and Women's Junior Formation Colloquium held at Gethsemani Abbey, Kentucky; to Patrick LaBelle and the priests of the Archdiocese of Portland, Oregon; and to the school of Applied Theology, Berkeley, for their help and support.

Contents

1

Introduction to Metaphor in Psalm and Parable

*T*he psalms are and have traditionally been the prayer book of Jewish and Christian communities. For that claim to remain true the psalms must speak to, for, and with us the reality we most want and need to express, and we need to recognize that the psalms "pray well" in us and we in them. There must be a fit that can deepen over time as the psalms help us identify our own experience and as they gain texture from our company.

That praying communities have used the psalms for prayer and worship is not difficult to document. Many still do, including those who meet to celebrate Jewish festivals and those who undertake the charge of praying the daily liturgy of the Christian church. But it is just as easy to demonstrate that for many prayerful believers, probably in both traditions but surely among Christians, the psalms have little appeal, are "hardly representative of the Catholic world as a whole . . . have not entered deeply into the prayer life of the faithful," to use the words of Cistercian commentator Matthew Kelty. He continues: "The reason is not hard to see. Most people do not consciously live on the level of the psalms. Consequently, they do not find the psalms true. They find them archaic, extremist, dramatic, overwrought, frantic. Many people do not pray the psalms because they simply do not feel the way the psalms feel."[1] We may assume or discover that we live in a wholly different world from the one the psalms inhabit and construct. Then the psalms will not be ours nor will we be theirs: a mutual loss.

The parables of Jesus are more accessible to most Christians; they seem easier to understand. Many consider them to be Jesus at his best and most appealing. Without countering such opinion, I would suggest another layer of challenge. The parables are often incipiently or inadequately understood, or perhaps so well worn that it is difficult to consider them afresh. We have heard them and listened to them preached so many times that we feel we know them, that they have little left to show us. So without our quite realizing it they slide into the category of the banal and redundant. We retire them, consciously or unconsciously, and they are no longer working for us, or we with them. They recede from our lives, I would suggest, without our really having come to know them very deeply at all, let alone exhausted them.

Besides this we are more likely to take them as example stories and allegories than to let them function as parables. The distinction between the labeling job that allegory does and the more complex transaction of working with parable is similar to the difference between scrutinizing a butterfly pinned to a board with its anatomical portions neatly and correctly labeled and watching such a creature in graceful motion. Allegory invites us to look for similarities between one referent or situation and another and to transfer them effectively; a parable is a narrative metaphor—a metaphor in motion—that by the peculiar working of its juxtaposed elements startles the mind into fresh awareness. Allegory is easier, more certain; parable is more dynamic and evanescent. Scholars have spent a good deal of time trying to classify Jesus' short narratives into types: allegory, simile, metaphor, parable. It may be more to the point for us to decide what reading strategies we will use for them and to resist reducing them all to examples of behaviors.

The stories Jesus tells do provide challenging examples for us, and some of them have allegorical features and potential. It may be most apt for us to do the same thing for poor people that the Samaritan does for the beaten and robbed person (Luke 10:33-35): act with compassion and minister to evident needs. But to allow stories like the Good Samaritan to function as parables, to interact with parables of Jesus, is quite a different thing from reading them more statically. If the parable of the Good Samaritan metaphorically redescribes our world we may be shown a slightly or substantially different scenario from the one confronted by the characters in that recital. If we do not allow for such a possibility, once again with all the best intentions in the world we hobble the texts, or rather cut ourselves off from effective use of the wonderful resource that the parables are in our tradition. So by two separate pathways we may end up in essentially the same place with both psalms and parables: they do not work very well for us in our relationship with God and the various communities we inhabit.

These studies represent an effort to reposition us before some psalms and parables so that we can meet them anew and they can function more usefully for us than may have been the case before. My experience both with myself and with many people I know is that we want very much to explore in language and experience the mysteries of God and our own human condition. We would like some help on the journey—perhaps a narrative of others' discussion of their own wanderings and sojournings—or perhaps we recognize that we already have "the book" but would like to get a little more help from it. It is just such companions that I have in mind here. With the assistance of eight psalms from what is called Book 1 (Psalms 1–41) of the whole book of 150 psalms, and with eight parables from what is called the travel narrative of Luke's gospel (roughly chapters 9–19, as Jesus moves from Galilee toward Jerusalem), let us see what we can do and how we can do it. Insight and the grace of deeper relationship with God and with all of creation are given as well as achieved, offered to us in many ways beyond our knowing; but it is important, even crucial, that we understand how some of our own reading skills and strategies can help us lay effective groundwork for whatever God may be collaborating with us to accomplish.

One strategy I have found very useful is to recognize that the psalms and parables often share the architecture and dynamics of metaphor. That is, part of what makes them work effectively is that they are coiled to do a job of redescribing some reality for us so that we see it slightly differently and are ourselves in some way changed. Metaphor can be a complex topic and we may bring to it mixed associations from various realms of our past, but if we can allow it to open some of its pathways for us we will be able to harness from the workings of metaphor some very practical possibilities for reading and prayer.

THE WORKINGS OF METAPHOR

A metaphor consists in the juxtaposing of two elements that share some basic congruence: the characteristics of one set are now seen as appropriate—or dissonant—for the other.[2] Another way to say the same thing is by using the image of screens. We sieve the characteristics of one realm through the screen of a different one, watching to see what suits and what does not, and why. Far from simply classifying what we already know, the metaphor pushily and invasively issues an invitation to reconsider such knowledge in a fresh light, putting our certainties at risk in the process but also inviting us into new worlds. So before turning to the eight psalm and parable texts that not only share a metaphoric structure but utilize common specific figures, let us spend a little time on theory.

There is a useful chapter in a book discussing characters in Luke's gospel that explains the process well.[3] Its author, John Darr, draws to our attention the place in Luke's travel narrative (specifically at Luke 13:32) where Jesus, alerted to Herod's intent to kill him, calls Herod a fox:

> Go and tell that fox for me, "Listen, I am casting out demons and performing cures today and tomorrow, and on the third day I finish my work. Yet today, tomorrow, and the next day I must be on my way, because it is impossible for a prophet to be killed outside of Jerusalem." Jerusalem, Jerusalem, the city that kills the prophets and stones those who are sent to it! How often have I desired to gather your children together as a hen gathers her brood under her wings, and you were not willing!

Darr explains at greater length than I will do here that what happens with metaphor, and with this one in particular, is that the whole semantic range of "fox" is brought into relationship with the whole semantic range of "Herod the king." Features of one realm—fox—catch or interlock with aspects of the other realm—Herod the king. The term "King Herod" is sometimes called the "subject" (or "tenor") while the reference "fox" is called "symbol" (or "vehicle"), suggesting that what we really want to discuss is the subject Herod and what will help us to do so is our catching some rays from the symbol of a fox. In reality it does not divide quite so cleanly, but the terms can be convenient to recognize. There is actually mutual illumination of both terms as we consider each in the light thrown by the other.

What Jesus' original listeners were challenged to do and what we ourselves need to do is ask what more we can learn about Herod—and about Jesus and even about ourselves—as we consider which foxlike qualities fit Herod well, which do not, and why. For purposes of clarity I will chart the process of entering the metaphor's dynamics in seven sequential steps, but the reader is encouraged to find his or her own pathways through the process of working with textual images. I am simply slowing down the process here almost artificially so we can see what kind of analysis can be undertaken in order to let the metaphor have some scope in our imaginations.

Step One: First in the process of working with metaphor is the clear identification of its elements or terms. Since we understand intuitively and correctly that Jesus knows even when calling him a fox that Herod is in fact a human being, we are in the presence of a figure, in this case a metaphor. It is a comparatively simple one and can show us metaphoric structure and possibilities fairly easily as well as introducing us to the context of Luke's long parable section. In some instances, including most of the figures to be worked with in the pages to follow, the subject and symbol are quite clear; but in at least two instances a significant part of the challenge of reading is to identify and articulate the terms of the metaphor. The simplicity of this example—both the obviousness of the figure and the cleanness of the two terms—can serve as a reference when we deal with metaphors that are submerged amid many other details.

Step Two: We inevitably and most appropriately start with our own experience of foxes and kings whether we recognize ourselves to be doing so or not. And even if we can claim little direct experience of vulpines or royals, in fact we will have a set of associations if we cast around for them. Awareness of our presuppositions is an important part of our reading and interpreting. If we are reading with others or praying with them the sharing of experience and information will show us a great deal. We will quickly see both a common core of material about foxes and kings on which we can agree but also perhaps more on which we may not agree at all, our experience being diverse. There will not be a single, clear "right answer" for the meaning offered by the meta-phor though some insights will be closer to likelihood than others.

I will merely suggest some possibilities here for purposes of illus-tration. Readers will easily find their own relevant associations. If we are fond of Antoine de Saint-Exupery's *The Little Prince* we will respond differently than if we have just read Frederick Forsythe's *The Day of the Jackal.* If we have seen most of our foxes at the zoo where we mostly pity them we may begin our interpretation differently than if we are sheep ranchers in Montana and find foxes the opponents of our livelihood, or if we are fond of riding with the hounds after our quarry, the fox.

Similarly when I had responsibility for a group of North American college students during several summers in Oxford the occasional days we spent in the company of a British bus driver named Colin and the opportunity to come to know an Oxford "scout" called by all of us "Mrs. B.," each of whom held the British royal family in some considerable affection, have given me a much more sympathetic view of monarchs than I would otherwise have had. But my reading of the history of British India suggests to me as well that over time the peculiar concentration of power comprising monarchy tends to be corrosive of justice. The simple juxtaposition of many conversations with these two working class British people and my own more theoretical opinion happily impedes oversimplification. The variables available to us from our own and others' lives are endless—and valuable. Hence early in dealing with a metaphor it is important to reflect on our own experience for whether we acknowledge it or not, that is where our understanding is rooted. As we do this step we will already be wondering whether Herod is going to emerge as an attentive and teachable, benign if paternalistic ruler or as a relentless predator.

Step Three: We continue our exploration of the two realms our metaphor has brought together. We can build up our catalogue of kings and foxes not only from initial soundings of our own experience but from other sources as well. Foxes live in dens or thickets, are furry, seem adept and smart, and act rapaciously—at least from a human perspective. They might, if consulted, have another name for their process of gathering food and yet another for our own ways of feeding and clothing ourselves. Foxes seem able to proceed silently and thus appear furtive, perhaps sometimes cowardly. Their powerful jaws make them appear dangerous. Their sleek and attractive bodies are often aesthetically appealing.

We may next ask and need to inquire how foxes were understood at the time of the writing of Luke's gospel, and of course we may consider the information from more than one viewpoint. Shepherds may have reacted differently to foxes than did tax collectors. We need to consider the presumed original audience(s) of Jesus and Luke as well as ourselves. The point is not to try to go back in a time capsule and become first-century Judeans, but neither is it sufficient to ignore the strong possibility that the assumptions of two thousand years ago will be different from our own—presumably in a helpful way. That last point reminds us of the importance of not assuming that our perceptions are normative. They are ours and legitimate, but they need not be anyone else's, especially insofar as our circumstances might diverge radically from those of first-century fox-experiencers.

We can run through a similar process for kings, probably even more alert to the differences occasioned by twenty centuries of time and by the fact that most of us live in a democracy where leaders are elected while the Palestinian regions of Jesus' time knew life under an emperor and his local, appointed king or delegate. Did ancient monarchs unfailingly live off the bounty of their people, taking much and giving little? Is Herod more a type than an individual, the metaphor more social than individual? There is some specific information about the Herod in question here, not only in but outside the gospels.[4]

Step Four: Our general historical inquiry will lead us closer to the specific texts themselves where we can examine the conventions involved and presumed for the metaphor and the contexts in which it is set. What is to be understood when we liken human beings to animals? How can we think about what we are doing when we mix human and animal categories, a practice quite common even in urban cultures where the animal population is restricted? The likening of human beings to fauna is a complex and intriguing code yielding considerable insight about us, if not them—but probably about them too, at least from the human perspective. What is the gain when we convert our rational, articulate *homo sapiens* identity into types that do not practice speech and rational discourse to any extent, at least so far as we know? What particular human edges come into greater prominence and which recede? What do we assume to be the process, the givens, as we (or Jesus) verbally revision people as animals? Is it physical appearance? behavioral traits? Is such use of metaphor a form of caricature? Is it pointed ears or a sharp nose that make Herod most resemble a fox or some moral quality? Are some animal ascriptions more complimentary than others? Are our perceptions about animal behavior rooted in reality or in some protective projection we may make? Is there something noble or appealing about the fox going silently, singly, and efficiently about its task? Is that what we sense about a king?

We need also in this step to look at the contexts in which the figure is used. Jesus is the one to utter this particular metaphor and he speaks it at a particular point in his journey to Jerusalem. Again we may sketch a few possibilities for exploration: the advice that triggers Jesus' fox comment is about going or journeying. Those warning Jesus tell him he needs to hustle quickly out of Herod's territory. Jesus, already "on the way" for purposes known to himself, to God, and shared at least partially with the reader, is advised to hurry along lest he be eliminated by

Herod. Jesus is thus prompted to make a comment about "goings" and "dyings," a statement suggesting the powerlessness of Herod at least in certain spheres. Jesus' assertion implies that Herod may not be so much in the know as he thinks nor so powerful an actor as he is envisioned to be either by himself or by the well-wishers who are tipping Jesus off about apparent danger. The poignant description of Jesus' own futile efforts to gather chicks under a wing is not unrelated to the fox image. So we may be seeing—or being shown—a Herod who is a powerless predator, a threatening but tethered tyrant not particularly shrewd or canny for all his trappings. On the other hand the quick and undeveloped reference to straying chicks discloses for us a glimpse of Herod from the angle of the more vulnerable.

We go back in Luke's gospel and see what we have been told and shown of King Herod so far, and of foxes as well, though there may not be much there. How is Herod drawn? What does he say? do? What do others say about him? Who says it? Is it said approvingly or not? With such questions and others like them we sketch a small profile of Herod, assuming that a literary artist like Luke will be reasonably coherent in the characterization of the man. Herod has had a few references in Luke's gospel before Jesus calls him a fox. We have encountered him as a dynastic ruler in 3:1, related to a man of the same name in 1:5. He has been linked by Luke to John the Baptist: John's ministry is first dated in terms of Herod; Herod next imprisons John when rebuked by him; and finally Herod kills John. When we hear the king rifling through his memories in an effort to puzzle out the identity of Jesus, the murder of John seems like simply a piece of data Herod uses in a process of elimination: "John I beheaded; but who is this about whom I hear such things?" (Luke 9:7-9). His casualness seems frightening, his power great. How Herod will continue to be characterized in the rest of the gospel and in the Acts of the Apostles (where he is referred to, other relatives having taken over his job) is relevant as well. The fact that Luke consistently portrays John the Baptist and Jesus in parallel frames is ominous. Herod, who killed John, threatens to do the same to Jesus. So the possibility of the rapacious, powerful predator emerges again. The simple metaphor of Herod as fox is supple and complex, serpentine and devious, very rich.

Yet, strangely but surely important to notice, Jesus has compared himself to a fox as well, contrasting his own itinerant situation and that of his disciples with the fox who at least has a hole to which he may go to rest or hide (9:58). If hunted, or when weary or sated from foraging, the fox can go to ground. Jesus indicates that such security or protection is not available to him. As should be clear, there are many strands to disentangle. To be complete is not necessary or possible, though to uncover a good range of possibilities makes for rich reading.

Step Five: We finally see what we have discovered as we slide the two realms into relationship, sorting everything we have learned about foxes through the screen of all that we know of King Herod. Though we cannot stop ourselves from doing the converging of the metaphor's terms virtually from our moment of recognizing that we are in its presence it can be useful to catalogue what in fact we have found, lest something valuable slip by unnoticed in the rush of insights. We see the kingly fox or the foxlike king surely as a predator, frightening in his power. He is at least to some extent shrewd and strategic, using his power to gain his own ends that have been destructive of the life and mission of at least one man; and since Herod's power is structural, not simply personal, we can see that the menace persists. We have the sense of the fox as pursuing prey not really in a secretive way but overtly, its presence not much needing to be camouflaged. There is an arrogance in the power that may command a grudging acknowledgment from those whose position is threatened.

Hence we also notice when sorting this figure that Jesus, if not those who warn him, minimizes some of the royal power. Though fearing for the straying chicks Jesus does not acknowledge the sovereign's power in his own life as completely as the circumstances might suggest. Without diminishing the negative qualities of the monarch, Jesus deflates the power Herod seems able to muster. The rapacious fox may miss his prey.

Step Six: The arranging of the features of the metaphor leads almost automatically and inevitably to the sorting of what fits and what does not. Our first effort seems easy and obvious. We may decide in this case that physical characteristics are not germane; Jesus does not call Herod a fox primarily because he resembles one physically. The tawny and sleek pelt of the fox is not what makes it comparable to the king. The appeal of the hunted fox, the pity generated by a trapped animal, are also to be discarded. The benignity possible in leadership, the shrewdness that can accompany and promote excellence in human endeavors are also to be laid aside here. If the metaphor is not exposing Herod's appealing facets, what are we more probably being shown?

The place where the "fox screen" most catches the characteristics of the royal features is in destructive behaviors. Kings like foxes go after what they feel they must attain, plunder what they cannot live without. A fox may kill to survive and so may a king. Both may have to act covertly until they are in a position to stride boldly. Kings and foxes appraise inhabitants with whom they share space primarily in terms of their own needs. Insofar as they are powerful enough to effect their own desired ends they do so, ostensibly without allowing other considerations to impinge. Yet each may also have to be leery of a larger competitor, perhaps a predator though perhaps simply another agent, whose purposes may cross those of the vulpine kinglet. The naked power that King Herod has used against John the Baptist, beheading him on the basis of inconvenience, suits our assessment of a fox killing a small animal that gets in its way or may menace its own cubs.

But a third and arguably most valuable part of our sorting the newly matched qualities that do fit from those that do not is to look for what seems semantically impertinent but in fact works quite well once we consider more carefully. It is with the help of such unexpected qualities that we will get freshest and keenest insight into a metaphor that otherwise may seem almost unnecessary. So is there any aspect of the King Herod as fox metaphor that we can reconsider before we eliminate it?

Jesus, though naming Herod "fox" and describing himself as a hen almost futilely in charge of protecting her chicks, nonetheless dismisses the power of the fox to dictate the terms. Though alleging all the qualities of the fox that we have discussed and attributing them to Herod, Jesus nonetheless startles us by refusing to run before the predatory animal. He thus manages with the terms and functioning of the metaphor to call attention to the way and the place in which and the agency by which he himself will not die, prompting us of course to look for more likely information on those points. Thus we vacillate between this royal fox as powerful and impotent, tempted at one moment to place "strategically powerful" in the pile of characteristics that is most apt but almost simultaneously deciding that it does not fit Herod very well and is one of the pieces to ignore. How can a self-confessed hen not fear a prowling and hungry fox once she clearly indicates that she has spotted it? But perhaps in redescribing a king in this way—the predator that misses the prey—Jesus is saying about aggregates of royal authority, "look again."

Step Seven: Finally, it may be possible—even in this rather labored exercise involving a few short words—that we will have been surprised into some insight. Jesus is not "on the way" by himself nor is he the only character with something to figure out as he journeys. The quick repartee may show us something in Jesus' turning from Herod's pursuit of him to his own care and concern about "Jerusalem's chicks" who are exposed and far from the wings of the one who would shelter them. We may initially feel smug in that we do not identify much with King Herod; it is obvious from the conventions in the gospel that Jesus is meant to seem the more admirable to us. But Herod may not be the only referent of the metaphor.

If we are honest we may all too well understand the fox's and the king's felt need to eliminate those who oppose or threaten. There are ways to disable our opponents besides removing their heads. One advantage of doing at least some of our metaphor exploration in diverse groups is that we will get information from others we would be unlikely to come up with ourselves. We can probably all envision ourselves easily enough as stalked by a predator who does not wish us well, but we are, I think, less liable to see ourselves easily in the various ways in which we do something similar to others, whether it is a matter of unconscious unkindness to those with whom we live or the tremendous hardships worked by our standard of living on many citizens of the rest of the world, with all the possibilities lying between those extremes. If we are not at some point uncomfortable when doing metaphors we are skipping steps or ignoring facets of the figures that are presented for our scrutiny. What are the uses of power that itemize the value of others wholly in terms of our own needs for survival?

In any case there will be some gain of insight for us to store, though we must also recognize that we have barely scratched the surface of the possibilities of the figure in our own experience, scarcely begun to play with the contexts in the gospel or in the larger canonical Scriptures. No metaphor reading is ever finished, perfect, settled. When we have had authority over others, or been hungry, or cared for sheep we can go back and refigure the imagery afresh. Our experiences, such as they are, of being persecuted or persecutors, of being labeled well or poorly will all give us insight into the workings of this apparently simple figure. And once we are exploring the pathways that compose this figure and the many others Scripture provides we see ourselves more fully and have plenty of opportunity for conversation with God and others about the essentials of living fully.

If Scripture is to continue to be revelatory in our lives, as it is meant to be for us as well as for our biblical ancestors, we need to allow it some room to maneuver. Being the densely patterned and brilliantly told narrative of the many dealings of God with other human beings and them with God, it will offer many surprises. Its metaphors have the capacity to sidle up to us with apparent innocence because they interest us but do not immediately threaten us. They blindside us, suddenly disclosing to us something we might have screened out had we seen it coming; we may even be able to bury such data, but if we continue to work with these scriptural metaphors the ones about which we are most sensitive and that we presumably need most will butt up against us again. They offer us self-knowledge in good company, both with other fallible human beings and a compassionate God. Partly a matter for our mind and reason to puzzle out, they also can cut through to our hearts and so change our wills and habits, perhaps not in one huge shift but in many installments and treatments. Our lives are thus gently but irresistibly rechanneled to draw from and feed into the resources of a living and loving God. It is not simply a matter of seeing with the mind and then sending an order over to the will, but without knowledge of ourselves, without understanding to some extent how we have come by such insight I am not sure there will be sufficient deepening. At least such has been my experience.

If this process seems tedious and artificial or perhaps overly analytical it may be comforting to recognize that in our ordinary lives we race through it quickly all the time, since much of our language relies on the use of imagery. I am drawing it out here for two reasons: first to provide a sample of steps that can give wonderfully rich texture to what might otherwise remain flat; and second to be sure it is clear how fluid and unfinished our reading is, however fresh it will always remain. We can dart too quickly past possibilities we do not even see, and we can too quickly assume that we have gotten all there is to get. I am not suggesting that there is not a fairly clear and stable core of meaning associated with Herod the fox; I think there is. But when dealing with metaphor we will not be able to pinpoint the meaning narrowly or forever. The Scriptures offer us far more flexibility than we tend to take up, and it is important for the scope of our imaginative capacities to recognize that resource. We will change, and our viewpoints on things will shift as well.

So by way of conclusion let us simply gather a few strands of the fox–king metaphor: We see Jesus—and ourselves—drawing King Herod as the somewhat powerful predator stalking not only Jesus but presumably others as well: John the Baptist, conceivably those on the journey with Jesus, others who will for one reason or another get in the potentate's way. Though he may be in a certain sense wily and shrewd he is also cowardly and paranoid. Though informed on some matters he is lacking significant information. His threatenings of presumed opponents may work at a number of levels; he makes many of his subjects expendable for purposes of his own. Though his power is in one currency negotiable beyond a doubt, in another system it is enfeebled. Herod's conscious designs have little to do with the larger purposes of God and Jesus who will struggle to see that he does not thwart their projects completely. Yet we cannot be romantic about religious and spiritual realities overcoming too easily the teeth of the fox. The chicks in fact can only be sheltered so far by the wing of the mother even if they have been gathered there, a charge Jesus grieves that he has not been able to accomplish.

Once the lines are drawn we may feel ourselves caught in the middle, like a small animal in car headlights, not sure which side is ours. To offer us a moment of honest uncertainty is one of the most important feats of the metaphor. Herod the fox, after all, is simply doing what he needs to do to preserve his spot, his role, his sense of himself, not to mention his little kingdom. Foxes and kings have to eat, have to live, to survive as do we all. It is to some extent beneficial for the common good as well as his own that he avoid any kind of scenario that would involve Roman authority intervening in Galilee or Judea. Jesus, apparently lined up in the sights of the fox, chooses not to resist directly, not to go after the fox–king but to continue on with some tangential project of his own—and God's. Whether it is wholly clear to him what he needs to do is not perhaps evident; he suggests that he will die, and in Jerusalem as a prophet, apparently failing in the task of protecting those he loves. But his goal seems uncertain, less focused than Herod's objective. God's projects have their own wisdom and power but it usually seems a vulnerable sort. The fox is perhaps more attractive in some ways than its prey, its position more able to be rationalized. A single word used in relation to Herod drags a lot of possibilities about the rest of us in its train. We may prefer competent power to defenseless regrouping. We may find ourselves wanting to hire a fox-king for our side. It may not be our most proud moment, the pinnacle of our self-rated success. If and when we recognize that impulse the metaphor has offered us self-knowledge, compassion for others, and a powerful stimulus to a change of heart. The reigning of God, God's ongoing projects of love and justice, come closer to us and we to them.

One other point may be underlined; it is relevant here and at other places related to Scripture. Our postmodern era and its modes of criticism have exposed and will continue to reveal the undertow of Scripture and those who interact with it, to explicate the assumed and regnant values of the communities that generated the biblical text and those of us who continue to use it particularly for prayer and worship. Forged as it has been in the real lives of very human communities as well as in the heart of God, Scripture expresses its insights about the God–human–cosmic relationship in language that is partially inadequate. The imagery and assumptions of the biblical text are rather thoroughly patriarchal and thus can be very difficult for some to read. What may not bother us much may be a great deal more troubling to others we know, and we need to take this problematic aspect of the Bible seriously for their sakes if not our own. Some of the most dominant and highly prized symbolism of the Hebrew Bible sets the people of God over against enemies the texts consistently characterize as deserving of total destruction. Those particular roots can seem violent and inappropriate for our norming and forming ourselves as individuals and as a people. Similarly the crucible of post-Temple-destruction Jewish and Jesus-committed struggles and the contention that characterized the first century leaves in many New Testament texts an anti-Jewish residue. Part of our reading will involve our attention to these aspects of reality as they interact, perhaps painfully and harmfully but probably helpfully, with our own experiences. We will learn a great deal.

So we will proceed more or less in this fashion—though I hope with the process not intrusive or so visible—to play with eight metaphors that are shared by a psalm and parable each. Psalm 1 and Luke 13:1-9 share the image of the rooted tree (Chapter Two). Psalm 8 and Luke 15:11-32 tell us about stature or status (Chapter Three). Psalm 27 and Luke 18:9-17 explore some possibilities of searching faces (Chapter Four). The lengthy Psalm 18 and Luke's brief tale in 18:1-8 disclose some things we need to know about entitlement and responsiveness (Chapter Five). Psalm 7 and Luke 16:1-9, perhaps the most difficult of all the parables of Jesus, offer us the image of moral ecology (Chapter Six). Psalm 23 and Luke 15:1-7 are among the many biblical texts that discuss the process of being shepherd and sheep (Chapter Seven). Psalm 39 and Luke 12:16-21 invite us into the stuffed storehouse to see what we recognize (Chapter Eight). Finally, Psalm 41 and Luke 10:29-37 will offer us insight about the other side, perhaps about sides in general (Chapter Nine). We will then conclude with a synthesis.

As we work with these very rich figures readers are encouraged to use my insights as suggestive and partial and to rework material here into other configurations in an effort to make these prayers and reflections their own. Though this introductory chapter may continue to serve as a useful schema throughout the rest of the book I will avoid working it like a checklist. Metaphors are really very familiar to us once we think about it, and we will need little instruction in how to cope with them once we have gotten started.

NOTES: CHAPTER 1

[1]Matthew Kelty, O.C.S.O., "The Psalms as Prayer," *Sermons in a Monastery. Chapter Talks* (Kalamazoo: Cistercian Publications, 1983) 10.

[2]The subject of metaphor can be arcane, rising as it does from the complexities of human language capacity and speech. Possibly the most influential theorist who both draws deeply but comes clearly to the point as well is Paul Ricoeur. His clearest writings on the subject can be found in *The Rule of Metaphor: Multidisciplinary Studies of the Creation of Meaning in Language* (London: Routledge and Kegan Paul, 1978) though his later works return to the topic as well. Another detailed treatment can be found in Sallie McFague, *Metaphorical Theology: Models of God in Religious Language* (Philadelphia: Fortress, 1982).

[3]John A. Darr, *On Character Building: The Reader and the Rhetoric of Characterization in Luke-Acts* (Louisville: Westminster/John Knox, 1992) ch. 5. His presentation of the Herod the fox metaphor was foundational to the insights I developed.

[4]There are four "Bible Herods." The Herod, more distinctively and properly named Antipas, who appears during the adult life of Jesus is not to be confused with his predecessor of the same family who threatened the life of the infant Jesus in the Gospel of Matthew nor with the petty magnates appearing briefly in Acts of the Apostles (chapters 12 and 23). The Herod in question here is referred to in Matt 14:1-6; Mark 6:14-22, 8:15; Luke 3:1, 19, 8:3, 9:7, 9, 13:31, 23:7-15. In addition to the brief comments about Herod found in the gospels, Josephus, the evangelists' contemporary, gives information about him in *Antiquities of the Jews*, 15–17. (See *The Works of Josephus*, trans. William Whiston [Peabody, Mass.: Hendrickson, 1987]). For reliable information about what the Jews of Jesus' time are likely to have thought about kings consult E. P. Sanders, *The Historical Figure of Jesus* (London: Allen Lane, Penguin Press, 1993) 42–43.

2

The Rooted Tree: Psalm 1 and Luke 13:1-9

*W*e begin our adventure of reading biblical metaphor with the first psalm of the psalter, set by the ancients as an overture to the many that follow. To accompany it and collaborate with it we choose an image, a metaphor that appears frequently in Jesus' teaching in Luke's gospel, a classic in all of his teaching: the fruit-bearing tree or its opposite, the non-productive plant. Though slightly more complicated than our example of King Herod as an animal, this metaphor of the tree as descriptive of our human lives will nonetheless take us on a journey of insight much as did the figure of the fox–king. The choice of the tree and the pairing of these two particular texts is rather obvious since both are explicit about the figure and its potential to teach us about ourselves. In other cases the discerning of the metaphor may be more a matter of deciding which of the possibilities of figurative language we wish to follow. The process of relating texts is similar to the opportunity the lectionary presents to us daily and weekly as portions from the two testaments are laid side by side for us to compare and interrelate.

The tree is for us an image with which we are comfortably familiar since virtually all of us live with trees. To shake loose our tree experience is a helpful entree to the two texts at hand. We may be fortunate enough to live where trees thrive, plentiful and healthy, or perhaps where they are few and survive against the odds. Our childhood may have been spent in company of a large and leafy tree that received us into its branches when we needed to hide, that sheltered us in games we wished to invent. Trees may have brushed at our windows and frightened us at night, and they may have been witness to our tears and angers. But we know trees or have plenty of opportunity to be sure we do. The planted tree and related variations serve as the metaphor here, working well in some ways to describe a human existence, not so well in other aspects. But the psalm and the parable offer us the image for our consideration: how does the tree work to redescribe our existence for us? What can we learn from it about the ways of God in our lives, the ways of ourselves in God's orchard or garden?

Though we can begin almost anywhere and can choose to circle in and out of texts as need arises and the metaphor beckons, let us begin this time with the parable, recalling that before we get to the metaphor we need to position the texts a bit first. As I suggested when we tracked the image of Herod the fox, there is no single rigid or unvarying method to apply to the texts; we will visit the seven steps that were helpful in our sample metaphor but leave many facets of the tree and other metaphors for subsequent exploration. The essays here are really little more than sketches to stimulate further creativity from us as we revisit these texts many times. Luke, like ourselves, provides some context for Jesus' parable about the tree. The gospel narrative says:

> At that very time there were some present who told [Jesus] about the Galileans whose blood Pilate had mingled with their sacrifices. He asked them, "Do you think that because these Galileans suffered in this way they were worse sinners than all other Galileans? No, I tell you; but unless you repent, you will all perish as they did. Or those eighteen who were killed when the tower of Siloam fell on them—do you think that they were worse offenders than all the others living in Jerusalem? No, I tell you; but unless you repent, you will all perish just as they did" (Luke 13:1-5).

So our reflection begins with some people arriving breathless to report or speaking up indignantly to remind Jesus about an episode of sacrilege, scandal, outrage. The Roman procurator or governor, Pontius Pilate, killed some people who were offering sacrifice, in effect turning them into sacrifices as well, mingling the blood of the offerers with that of the offerings. Though not attested elsewhere in historical record the act described is horrific, offensive, and would have been politically explosive in the Roman-occupied and permanently volatile region of the Middle East. It is not difficult in our own era, familiar with savage deeds perpetrated against groups, to understand the situation.

But Jesus in his typically non-predictable way does not immediately sympathize with the victims or excoriate the imperial perpetrator. Rather he poses a question back and then raises the speakers' current event by one. "Do you think their tragedy singles them out as particularly deserving?" we understand (and paraphrase) him as asking. "What about those who chanced to be in the line of collapse when part of a poorly-constructed tower fell: are they worse than other sinners on whom a tower did not fall?" He picks up on an inference drawn or suspicion held by those who tell him about the tragedy, on a point they do not quite make, either because he suspects they are thinking of it or because he thinks it is the point that needs thought. Big suffering equals big sin?

As soon as the equation is out in the open I suspect we begin to back away from it and deny it. We know better than that, and we are correct. It is not safe or wise to infer an instance of crime from the visible effects of punishment. But let us consider the linkage of sin and suffering again through the eyes and ears of people we know, if not quite through our own categories of experience or belief. The assumption is that there is a rough justice meted out in the universe: people we know often get what is coming to them, reap the results of their own choices. Many, many people feel that God settles scores with the wicked—whether they be our opponents or ourselves—and many think as well that often such divine retaliation is easy to spot, simple to parse. So we may sense that there is something wrong with the question Jesus is placing: when tragedy strikes people does it have something to do with what they deserve? But if we are listening afresh we are not quite so sure as we were a minute ago just what is wrong with the logical arrangement of cause and effect.

And then Jesus really throws us off by saying to those who have reported the Pilate event to him, "If you do not do something about turning away from wickedness and toward God you will perish too!" (Luke 13:5). He now seems to be saying the very thing he niggled at when his conversation partners posed it: sin brings on suffering, suffering is rooted in sin: "Watch out, big sinners, else big perish!"

We may at this moment stop and think about a particular textual convention that is difficult to discern from written material, and that is tone. Is Jesus scolding here, or almost teasing? Is he brushing aside a genuine concern some have brought him or is he reaching out to engage the problem brought, but simply at a deeper level? Each of us needs to consider what we think about the nonverbal aspects of the scene we are overhearing from the gospel and we need to think about that question of the mood in which Jesus engages his companions, perhaps reaching around in our own experience for analogues. The tone, the facial expression, the many facets of engagement that we are not told matter significantly in communication. We need to make our near-automatic or well-trained and quickly-heeling assumptions more explicit to ourselves.

I suggest as helpful and likely that we assume that Jesus enjoys conversations about important issues, loves to talk with people about what will bring them—us—closer to God. Such discussion is, in fact, his favorite pastime because he loves God deeply and wants to help us to do so as well. The parables are, among other things we may discover about them, invitations Jesus sketches for us to encourage and welcome us to live in God's realm. The psalms are, in addition to other attributes we will uncover about them, well worn and beloved scraps of conversation exchanged between God and people like us in moments of great intensity.

But Jesus is also like an athlete, let us say a lover of tennis, to whom we (or the characters in the texts) somewhat halfheartedly or shyly hit a ball across the net. We get a real game from him because it is more satisfying that way. He does not dismiss our ambivalent lob of the ball as though we were too unworthy for him to play, nor does he cream us in order to prove his own superiority. But we get a workout because that is how to enjoy and benefit from a game of tennis. The Judaism of Jesus' time was full of intensive conversations among people about issues just like the one we have before us. Like ourselves, the members of the various Jewish communities engaged each other energetically in order to come to greater insight on key questions like justice and repentance, the relationship between divine prompts and human preferences. Vigorous debate is fun and fruitful, and it clarifies positions and choices. So let us get involved with this one ourselves.

Thus when we come bringing our scoop about "the others," their shortcomings, and our hunches about justice, Jesus simply shifts the actors from "the others" to ourselves—probably not a bad idea—and then underlines the equation we do not quite say. What is the question he has placed on the table for debate, about which he has twice asked us for our opinion: "What do you think?" It is no longer simply or primarily about Pontius Pilate or Galileans, but ourselves and the way we live our lives and interact with our own family, friends, communities, neighbors, fellow inhabitants of the planet. We do not hear from the speakers in this section again, as though Luke nods to us that we are "on" now instead of them. Perhaps they feel sent off with a flea in their ear or in high dudgeon, indignant that Jesus does not seem to want to agree that Pilate is a tyrant. I prefer to think that they enjoyed and benefited from the exchange; Luke has simply erased their particular version of it, as it were, so that we can feel encouraged to engage Jesus ourselves. If we stay on for the conversation, for further exchange with Jesus, what is a likely trajectory of our discussion?

The question he poses for us, helps us to see we need to be asking, is this: What are we doing, who are we, and how does it relate to what is happening to us? It sounds abstract but will lose that quality as soon as we fill in with an example from our own particular circumstances. We may be confronted suddenly by a serious illness in the midst of our productive lives. Or we may be the victim—perhaps even the unwitting or casual perpetrator—of a serious injustice. We may be in the wrong place when thieves or terrorists make their moves that suddenly affect us intimately. Things happen; thinking of the events in our lives that are not unlike the gruesome deed of Pilate and the crashing and crushing tower are not difficult. Our lives and those of people we know are intersected by unexpected and undeserved events all the time.

If we expect Jesus to deny causality, as he seems to be on the verge of doing when he asks if we considered the ones suffering grievously to be big sinners, he may disappoint us when he tells us to hurry our own moral inventories lest we end up with towers falling on us too! And this exchange occurs in a section of Luke's travel narrative where the topic is the weather and reliable indicators of it (12:54-56). So what do events tell us about causes, the outsides communicate about the insides, our lives about our hopes and beliefs, our "profits" about our "investments"?

With the topic thus clarified thanks to this introductory context from Luke's travel narrative, let us begin the exploration of the metaphor of the tree, which is where Jesus heads the gospel conversation. A psalm, though, will help us to get going on it.

> If you would be happy:
> never walk with the wicked,
> never stand with sinners,
> never sit among cynics,
> but delight in the Lord's teaching
> and study it night and day.
> You will stand like a tree
> planted by a stream
> bearing fruit in season,
> its leaves never fading,

its yield always plenty.
Not so for the wicked,
like chaff they are blown by the wind.
They will not withstand the judgment,
nor assemble with the just.
The Lord marks the way of the upright,
but the corrupt walk to ruin (Psalm 1).

The psalm helps us specify options, pick ourselves out from a lineup, which as we will see is one of metaphor's favorite strategies. Happy—blessed, doing well, to be congratulated—are those who do not do three things: walk with serious evildoers, stand around with smalltime crooks, sit and deliberate with those who have no interest in even trying to be moral. Walking, standing and sitting approach presenting a fairly apt description of how we spend our time, and big-time villains, petty offenders, and moral dropouts (those who simply do not take seriously the struggle to live morally and justly) seem a representative cross section of our friends and others in and out of whose lives we dart. We should feel immediately right at home. And the psalm seems to pose something unlikely, if not impossible. Which of us does not spend a fair amount of time doing just those things with precisely such types? Again we can sort through our experience, pick an average day, and see how close the fit is. Some psalms, as we know or will discover, are minutely explicit about sins or crimes. Psalm One draws rather the general picture of us busily filling in our time walking, standing, sitting, leaving us to look carefully to discover the exact nature of the deeds so done. What exactly are we undertaking and with what result? Where is it getting us, all this activity?

What is the alternative, we may wish to know. The psalmist is ready to tell us. Rather "blessed" is the one who stands more independently, is absorbed in other realities, ruminates on something else. So the tree. Before we worry too much about the differences between people and trees let us see what they may have in common. What are the choices the metaphor of the tree presents to us here? The psalmist will draw two pictures and say: "Choose one."

As we first begin to match our general experience to that represented in this text and consider the tree it looks solid, still, substantial, stuck, fixed, passive—rather than walking on special missions, lingering in important dialogue, pulling up a chair for a confidential consultation. But the psalm specifies that the tree has been planted—is not simply a volunteer—and that it is responding, cooperating, sustained by something with which it is busy interacting. It sends out its roots to the water, draws water back to itself through those roots, distributes nutrients throughout its own miles-long system. The tree puts out foliage for animal habitations, stabilizes soil in which countless others live and on whom many depend; it produces fruit for hungry people like us—no matter what, the psalmist underlines. Far from inactive, it is fertile, fruitful, productive; first planted, it is now rooted.

The opposite image is the chaff: dry, separated, tiny, sterile, blown apart, disintegrating. It will not win in court, will lose its footing, will fly off unrooted until it is no more. Anyone who suffers from hay fever knows what chaff is. So the tree metaphor actually offers us two extremes of insight about how we choose to be active, tells us about spending our busy time in two different ways. So we toggle our vision in two directions: the thrumming tree, the scuttling chaff.

Choose, the psalmist invites us: do we want to be a tree or chaff? Which describes us best? We know, undoubtedly, what the right answer is; but it is not so easy! As we look again and reassess the chaff seems more mobile, flexible, busy, involved, participatory: walking, standing, sitting are the things that seem most to count, the actions that help us feel productive. The tree on the other hand is absorbed in Torah or God's instruction: ruminating on it, murmuring over it, humming the bars of it, whistling and singing it, tuned in to the channel or station of Torah as it goes leafily and fruitfully on about its life. The metaphor poses to us a choice that is not so easy, that is certainly automatic only at the most superficial glance. We begin to see more clearly that the choice of trees is not between action and inaction, between splendid isolation and contaminating collaboration, but is rather a question of absorbed in what? chewing on what? ruminating on what? planted where? producing what?

The psalmist drops us another major hint. The one meditating on the teaching or Torah of God finds it in the Hebrew language of the psalms *ḥapeṣ* the cognate English word through the Latin is "voluptuous." The tree, so to speak, finds God's instruction pleasurable, interesting, stimulating, fun—not tedious, boring, dull, disappointing. So the choice is between spending our allotment of time, whatever it may be, as one that God plants, tends, cares for, entertains and helps, or disbursing it in other ways that remain uninterested in God's instruction, wander off to perish, dry up, cease to be, disintegrate. It is important to note here that the psalmist does not say that God zaps or gets even with the one who chooses something else, but simply that such a choice is eventually, inevitably, persistently self-destructive for the chooser. The chaff, dried up, burns out. So the question the tree metaphor of Psalm One is posing to us comes at last into sharper focus: how can we prefer rootedness in God so that we will choose it? How can we consistently sink our roots ever deeper toward God, not as a chore or a consolation prize but as a genuine preference and deep desire? How can we acquire a thirst for God and find it slaked with fair consistency?

The essayist and novelist Richard Rodriguez has pointed out that in our era at least in certain parts of the United States we see many people going about their business almost absentmindedly carrying great flagons of water. Runners strap on designer canteens, roller bladers stop to refresh themselves from flasks, executives lift Evian bottles from supple briefcases, babies swig as they are strollered along. People even sit in aromatic coffee houses faced with nothing but a glass of water. Rodriguez metaphorizes this thirst, genuine concern as it is for healthy refreshment, as a desire for God. His provocative and gently humorous image fits the psalm's insight well. Busy about many things, whatever their quality, we come to know our thirst and reach to relieve it, or to let the water restore our parched selves. The planted tree, nurtured and healthy, manages refreshment better than does the chaff whose very motions wreak a desiccating havoc. The tree redescribes our lives in related alternatives, in points along a temporal spectrum. Let us shift back to the conversation Jesus has engaged us in—or we him—as it, too, now turns to the metaphor of the tree.

Luke continues:

> Then he told this parable: "A man had a fig tree planted in his vineyard; and he came looking for fruit on it and found none. So he said to the gardener, 'See here! For three years I have come looking for fruit on this fig tree, and still I find none. Cut it down! Why should it be wasting the soil?' [The gardener] replied, 'Sir, let it alone for one more year, until I dig around it and put manure on it. If it bears fruit next year, well and good; but if not, you can cut it down'" (Luke 13:6-9a).

So Jesus, like the psalmist, tells a story about a tree. All trees are not the same but again we know enough from our own tree experience to get the general idea. This is a fig tree planted in a vineyard, a pair who hang around together with fair frequency in Scripture.[1] "Planted," as we have already seen, implies the choice of someone at some time; but no choice can feel secure forever. This fig tree is not dry and flimsy and on its way to disintegration as is the chaff of Psalm One, but it is, or seems, stuck, sterile, and in trouble. It has gone nine years producing no figs if we calculate (based on what we have heard) three years for its growth, three more when any of its yield would be sacrosanct (according to Jewish law), and then three more years when the owner imagined he might be eating juicy figs but had enjoyed none.[2] So three years as a sapling, three years of windfalls for God, three more years of disappointment to all involved. The parable also draws our attention almost subliminally, as does the psalm, to the passage of time that comprises a life. The fig tree has not done bad things but it is not showing a yield for its time. What is worth spending a life on? the tree metaphor asks us.

The owner in Jesus' story notices. He has apparently been scrutinizing the dearth for some time; he sounds vexed, rushed, decisive, ready to chop. We may have the impression that this is not his first visit to the tree but rather that he is nearing the end of trips he plans to make to see how it is doing. He is growing impatient with the figless tree. And so the owner talks to the gardener in front of the tree. Such a tactic can seem to us demoralizing, intimidating, embarrassing, and we should assess it carefully in terms of various experiences we may have had, or we may think it bracing, challenging. How each of us construes the strategy of the owner—and that of the parabler—will depend on many variables within our experience. Those many and diverse moments when we have been scolded or bucked up by such a procedure as well as the occasions when we applied such measures to those for whom we felt responsible will come crowding forward in our memories as we interpret, and they will be influential. There is no point in not recognizing them, in fact significant value in letting them have some play. Our best work with these figures comes when we are most honest and most alert.

Listening to the words of the owner, the gardener is not taken aback. Knowing the tree as the one who has spent most time with it, the gardener is already prepared with a diagnosis and a plan. The tree, its cultivator suggests, needs time, needs tending. It may be root bound, the soil may be leached, there may be nothing for the tree to be sinking its roots into. The gardener, brown hands resting at the base of the fig tree, looking up from a kneeling position into the face of the owner, takes the part of the tree, cares for its way.

And we are not sure what comes next in the parable since this one, like many of the riddling narratives, stops "in the middle." The choice is similar to the one posed for us by the psalm: produce or perish! This time the owner—whom we need not rush to identify as God—says he will take a hand in the destruction of the fig tree, will not simply let it freeload in the valuable soil that could be nourishing a few more vines, will not wait until the tree gradually sloughs off into chaff. In the limited and carefully apportioned soil of the land at the end of the Mediterranean Sea there can be little patience with waste, little tendency to let a fig tree that is not able to meet its own obligations prevent an owner from squeezing out a little more space for a highly valued crop. Time seems crucial here, as it often does for those farming the earth. We may secretly hope or assume we can spend our salad days walking, standing, and sitting with shakers and movers and then retire to be contemplative trees. But the psalm and parable suggest perhaps not; we had best not count on it. Walking, standing, and sitting without pleasurable instruction may be sufficiently harmful to our health that by the time we schedule in our conversion we are already irreversibly on the way to chaff. Even if we might ascertain just how many post-conversion days we could count on and how many are held in reserve for us until we request them there might still be something flawed in such reasoning. The parabler may be counseling us against planning a galvanizing retreat at the Siloam Center lest the tower fall just as we are uncapping our pens and opening our stiff new journals!

So the tree metaphor has helped us to think about our situation, and we make the comparison explicit as we slide together the human and arboreal realms of the metaphor: going how? planted where? enjoying what? roots snaking out toward which sort of soil? drawing back which nutrients and vitality? producing what? stuck where? resisting why? slipping off into wisps of irritation at whom, in what cause? We are brought to a point of choice. Shall we rush around busily? steep ourselves in Torah? vanish into nothingness? Do we find ourselves scolded and threatened, despite—or lacking—our best efforts, or in trouble and dosed with manure? The reliable and experienced hands of the gardener are resting gently on us, her eyes—or his eyes—on us while she or he speaks confidently, perhaps even at some risk.[3] The gardener is not comparing us with other trees nor are we feeling the need either to congratulate ourselves on superior attainments or to try to hide our inadequacies from anyone. There is not much point in such deception nor in our frenetic walking, standing, or sitting insofar as they are part of the way in which we shore up our own self-importance.

We may suddenly discover that the doing may not be mostly ours here. It is not what we organize and commandeer that matters. The gardener has something for us: manure, of all things! How unimpressive.

What conversation could be off limits as the gardener applies such a therapy to our condition? So we talk to the gardener who is talking with us, helping us to sink more healthily into the place where we are already planted, ensuring that we can get angled to draw on what we need and what is plentiful for us. The gardener is on our side, at our side, marks our condition and our potential, is eager to give us the one gift needful, confident that we will respond. As we can see, the ending is open. We will pass by, or founder at this particular place many times in our lives, each time prompted to choose afresh.

Before leaving this wonderful image let us consider a few other possibilities. A common reaction is to bridle a bit at the tree comparison, to feel justifiably that it is too passive an analogue for us. Trees who are just stuck there have little to do with our self-actualizing, responsible human selves, we may feel. And that is so. A tree is not on the fast track that we may find ourselves on, or wish to be on, or feel we can scarcely escape. The ingesting of Torah, contrasted as it is with other activities, may not look very relevant. To attend to the place where the metaphor pinches is an important source of insight. It may be that the part of the image that does not work well is the fact that the tree's apparent lack of mobility, its inability to make moral decisions, makes it a poor symbol for human subjects, a facet of the metaphor to be discarded.

But it is equally possible that this irritating rub is part of the truthful communication it subtly offers us. The tree may also remind us that we are less in charge than we may like to think. The very irritation we may feel when likened to a tree may reveal to us one of the problems that we are caught in: the illusion of our overweening importance, our self-sufficiency and potency. It is wonderful to be a human being but we may be less sovereign in relation to the rest of the universe, perhaps even to ourselves, than we like to think. To be seen in all the right places with just the right people makes a more impressive video for our careers than does a blunt conversation taped as we stand, silent and root bound, waiting to see what will be given us. A tree is very interdependent, receiving and giving. We may feel a little more in charge of our own destiny than is good for us. The tree metaphor asks us to ponder the possibility. What seems semantically clumsy or impertinent may, just as we are about to rise above it, catch us by the ankle and pull us back for a second look.

The insight that the challenge is to receive, to allow our roots to be provided with good things, may be the very twist that the metaphor has for us. Fatigued, discouraged, burned out, we may not want to struggle to be good trees; but that is not what we are being asked to do. We need (to shift the image) to bask in the water table, not dig and fill it first or constantly. The trees, healthy and thwarted, invite us to ponder our capacities for receiving as well as giving, for reabsorbing vitality as well as promoting it.

The metaphor developing here also brings up the question of assessment: we judge the others, and they judge us. Some Galileans have secret suspicions about the evil of the others, Judeans are outraged by the behavior of the Roman governor, a vineyard owner seems disdainful and impatient over the nonfruitfulness of the fig tree. The parables always invite us to play all the roles. We do not care to be judged but we are not averse to passing the occasional judgment on others. Jesus, not unfamiliar with any human dilemma, cuts through our hinted accusations of the others and says: "What about yourself?" He need not say it unkindly, and he seems rather to speak like the vineyard owner or the gardener. It is a matter of urgency to turn the toes deeper into the rich soil that has a good deal to offer. Hardship will come—bad weather, demanding merchants, predators—but the tree is not set so shallowly that it will be easily thrown off by those things. The tree does not like these potentially destabilizing events and situations and neither do we, but we need not inevitably find them devastating. The drought can drive our roots deeper down toward what is there, can help us hum the voluptuous melody of God's Torah more resolutely—to employ our old phrase from the psalm.[4]

The tree metaphor is pervasive in Scripture, related to the various ways in which God as farmer, gardener, and vinegrower labors with us. It is a close relationship, an intimate one we know from our own participation as planters, growers, arrangers of produce. The roles are distinct but the project is common, collaborative. There are good days and discouraging ones, but the bond uniting the participants perdures. The gardener talks to the plants, loves being with them, invests consistently in their well-being, enjoys and benefits from the fruits. The plants presumably feel themselves lucky, blessed, to have such wonderful care. Who can but thrive with such a gardener?

The parables of Jesus—this one, the ones in the essays ahead, those in the gospel—all offer access to the reigning of God in the lives of believers. The realm of God, of which Jesus so frequently speaks in both prayer and teaching, is not fundamentally different from God's projects with the people Israel as brought to prayer and reflection in the psalms and other Hebrew Bible texts. A tree is part of a larger system: ecological, economic, sociopolitical, psychological, spiritual, physical. The tree shows us one version of our choices for participating in divine projects: digging in, reaching down deeper, stretching higher, putting forth what we can manage. We participate with appropriate energy, sustained by much of which we are scarcely aware, offering our fruits to many we will never see. Our own experiences with trees—as playful children, as perspiring gardeners, as determined builders, as carvers, as artists, as those in need of warmth—can lead us into many places of reflection and insight as we think about our roles in God's beloved land.

NOTES: CHAPTER 2

[1]The vine and fig tree are often paired in the parallelism of Hebrew poetry, e. g., Joel 1:7, 12; Mic 4:4. Together they represent Israel, God's people, and give the speaker and hearers of the texts opportunity to reflect on the relationship between the plants and the one tending them. So when Jesus seems almost casually to throw these terms together, in fact they already have a long tradition in the ears and hearts of his hearers. It is as though he is beginning a new chapter in a long serial.

[2]The detail that the owner may very well have had a nine-year wait is suggested by Kenneth E. Bailey, *Through Peasant Eyes* (Grand Rapids: William B. Eerdmans, 1980) 82. This is a sample of the rich detail available in commentaries.

[3]Though the gospel text assumes grammatically if not socio-culturally a male gardener, our own experience does not demand such a construal. One of the ways in which the familiar texts of Scripture can become fresher for us is by envisioning aspects the gospel leaves unexplored. This passage, whose central image involves a series of relationships "across species," does not require a male gardener. For some further possibilities see Loretta Dornisch, *A Woman Reads the Gospel of Luke* (Collegeville: The Liturgical Press, 1996).

[4]A wonderful resource for enfleshing these metaphors in unromantic reality is biography. How, for example, does a human being like South African Nelson Mandela emerge from twenty-seven years of brutal treatment in jail—that sentence mandated by a lifetime of constant racism—to love his opponent so steadfastly? He does not tell us directly but gives us a good deal of information for reflection in *Long Walk to Freedom: The Autobiography of Nelson Mandela* (Boston: Little, Brown & Co., 1995).

3

Stature: Psalm 8
and Luke 15:11-32

*H*aving examined ourselves within the set of identities offered
by trees we turn to something slightly more abstract but at
the same time more distinctively human: stature, or status, sig-
nifying our size and importance. Psalm 8, posing us artistically against
several backgrounds of the physical neighborhood of the universe, and
Jesus' most famous parable of the prodigal son work this common
metaphor of our size, one of the many ways in which both texts give us
access to the workings of the reigning or purposeful presence of God in
our lives. To state the metaphor clearly is key here: the various measures
of our "standing" fit both well and poorly our creaturely significance.
As we explore the parable in particular it will become obvious that in
no sense do these rich biblical texts reduce to the images we are examining here. Part of the depth and resilience of the Scriptures, one aspect
of their versatile gift to us, is that they have a virtually endless supply of
facets to share with us, proliferating as we see fresh combinations and
juxtapositionings with our lives. Every text under discussion here has
many more secrets to share with us as many times as we revisit them.

"Stature" or "status" may seem an odd place to begin as we look at
the two texts before us. What does the word pair provoke in us? Stature
reminds us that we can be weighed, measured, shod, gloved, hatted. If
we are playing basketball one stature is more useful than if we are settling into our economy class seat for a plane flight to Singapore. The experience of a plane trip reminds us also of some features of status. As

we crowd into the coach or economy section of the plane we cannot avoid passing those first-class passengers who are already settling into their more spacious leather recliners, their coats and jackets hung up carefully on hangers by those flight personnel not already preparing drinks. We have at once a lesson in both stature and status.

When teeing off at a Pebble Beach golf course we will see that some provision has been made for discrepancies in our gender-linked stature and strength and other perquisites have been designed with our status in mind. Though related, the words are not quite the same. The height of our head—our stature—may be one thing, but it may well be relative to what or whom we are standing beside. The type of hat we like to imagine perched on our pate to signify our status is a distinct but related issue: a crown? a miter? a capoose? a Paris fashion? a hard hat? the Oxford cap of an academic? a baseball cap, its bill hunched over the back of our neck? Stature is not in any sense an absolute, nor is status.

Perhaps as we sort our memories we remember a recurring day in elementary school when the mothers of our classmates or even our own mother came to weigh and measure us and reinscribe our permanent record cards with the numbers of our stature. Or maybe we as mothers had that charge and had to meet the distrustful or frightened eyes of the overweight or the undersized. Children and others seem to sense instinctively that some statures are more appreciated than others. A too-fat little boy or a too-tall little girl will not enjoy the day when stature is assessed. On the other hand, the day the basketball recruiter comes around with college scholarships the tall girl may feel better. Stature is relative.

Perhaps what we can see as we think about stature and especially as we think about the more complex topic of our status—the more intangible network of ways in which our "size" is reckoned by ourselves and others—is that criteria make all the difference. Some categories matter very much to us, some not at all. If we value being and appearing efficient our slip-ups and oversights will embarrass us; if we don't care much that we seem to be slick organizers we will scarcely notice the indications that we are inadequate in that particular context. Insofar as external appearances are vital to us, whether it be our clothes, our car, our address—where we live or what we are called—we will find it humiliating to fall short in these ways. If we take a good deal of pride in always looking suitably dressed we may find ourselves oddly irritated at those who drop in on us and find us sartorially sloppy. Since we obviously have the right to dress down if we are beating the rugs or mucking out a barn our spurt of anger may surprise us into a fresh insight about what our clothes are doing for us. If we like to be called "Doctor" it can be quite instructive to assess our feelings when some ignoramus omits the word or calls us by something less important. If such marks of status are less important to us we will find it easier to expose ourselves to others without them.

But it may be that we are not clear what we value or that we have some reason to hide from ourselves as well as from others the aspects of our status that we feel most strongly about. In that case certain things will set us off but the wiring will be crossed. That is, we will bridle at situations for no reason that is apparent to us, or we will mis-attribute our uneasiness to sources other than the true ones. We can learn a lot about our status and our own measuring and outfitting it by surprises that are presented to us. We have for the most part arranged our own "permanent record card" of our stature, the various measures we have for our status; we find that it works well enough for us, offers a suitable view for the others—or at least for our estimate of their appraisal of us! Our status includes our ways of talking about ourselves: how important we are, how appreciated or unappreciated; how feared we are and how fearful, how confident, how resentful or at peace. We hope that others will confirm our assessment and are even happier when they inflate it a bit or tell us we are too modest! We secretly agree.

In general I think we prefer to secure a size rather than have one that tends to expand or shrink back on us; in any case we prefer to manage our status ourselves and avoid radical, unplanned shifts. It is not easy to see our status altered, to sustain a correction, as is said of the stock market—but it happens, often for our benefit. And such gifts of resizing come in the psalm and parable we have before us. We may have had the trivial experience of putting a woolen sweater in the wash and retrieving it, now of suitable size for a child. Or we may struggle to fit inside belts whose faded secret inscriptions say "24" or "36," preferring a day of short breaths to the realization or admission that we are not so svelte as we once were or now desire to be. Such experiences can be funny when they happen with clothing but revealing nonetheless, and of more than inches. It can be more painful but perhaps more efficacious when it is our fuller selves rather than just our waistlines that have to face facts.

So the metaphor juxtaposing status or stature with our mostly non-quantifiable selves gives us an opportunity to size ourselves up, to measure what there is and what we may lack, to think about what we want and what we dread. Just as the fox metaphor fits Herod the man in some ways but not in others, and as the tree figure describes us in certain ways we may not have anticipated or even liked, so examining our size and assessing its significance allows us to appropriate some new insights. Let us this time examine the psalm and then, when finished, turn to the parable.

Psalm 8, a short poem about the very topic of our size, presents us with an unusually balanced and disciplined shape of its own. Not only the content but the very form of the psalm invites us to look at physical arrangement.[1] Many psalms sprawl more sloppily than does this one. Its careful proportionings, visible in its four layers of concentricity, invite us to find ourselves in its arrangement, to see just where we fit in. Let us look at it as well as read it.

> 2 *Lord our God,*
>   *the whole world tells*
>   *the greatness of your name.*
>   *Your glory reaches*
>   *beyond the farthest star.*
>   3 Even the babble of infants
>   declares your strength,
>   your power to halt
>   the enemy and avenger.
>   4 I see your handiwork
>   in the heavens;
>   the moon and the stars
>   you set in place.
>   5 What is humankind
>   that you remember them,
>   the human race
>   that you care for them?
>   6 *You treat them like gods,*
>   *dressing them in glory and splendor.*
>   7 You give them charge of the earth,
>   laying all at their feet:
>   8 cattle and sheep,
>   wild beasts,
>   9 birds of the sky,
>   fish of the sea,
>   every swimming creature.
> 10 *Lord our God,*
>   *the whole world tells*
>   *the greatness of your name.*

Some very general comments related to stature assisted by the variations in type will help us get going. The psalm is framed by verses 2 and 10 which are a repeating refrain. Their opening and closing of the psalm reiterate the topic: praise of God sung by creation throughout the cosmos. The center, roughly equidistant from both edges of the frame, offers both a repetition and an inversion: not only creation thinking of God, but God thinking of creation. More precisely, the central verses (vv. 4-5) picture ourselves imagining God envisioning us. The rest of the psalm details the realms where God's praise flows: in each case first the "far out" upper reaches of creation (vv. 2b, 6) and then the closer-up lower parts (vv. 3, 7-9). The psalm thus shows as well as says that placement, relative position, is worth our notice. As we move in closer to examine the structure more closely, symmetry and balance guide our investigation.

First the refrain. Setting the topic, it asserts, as we can see, the stature of God: the psalm offers top billing to God in the theater of the whole universe. God's name—which is to say God's self, reputation, credibility, and integrity—is huge, majestic, wide, noble, royal. The unified shout of all creation is God's name. The psalm begins and ends with that information, asserting that everyone knows and speaks about it, every creature expresses it continually. The psalm sets God's greatness as its primary measure.

Turning from the praised to the praisers though without ceasing to stress God's status, the poet begins now to measure with diverse rulers. First she[2] relates how the visible creation itself hardly begins to contain God's lavish glory; it overflows earth and heavens, seeping joyously into the cosmos, climbing beyond the grasp of the farthest star. The next size (v. 3) is quite small: we, though we babble like babies—our best words coos and goos—manage as well to speak of what God can do, how God can manage opposition. We may, the psalm suggests, strain our eyes and our necks, looking up to peer beyond God's farthest asteriate fingerwork glittering against the dark backdrop, but the psalmist assures us that even as infants, unspeaking ones, our praise to God is effective.

Skipping over the center of the psalm for the moment, we experience another dizzying shift in stature as we find ourselves regents of the cosmos (vv. 6-7). Though sucklings still, we are crowned. Small in the cosmos, we have responsibility, sharing in the clothes of glory and splendor that we praise in God. We have been made responsible for the world, the psalmist reminds us (though she speaks of "them" in the third person, we nonetheless recognize ourselves). The same creation that sings of God's name is placed by God at our feet, almost as a tribute. We enumerate our responsibilities in a pair of merisms: cattle, sheep (the large and small domesticated animals) as well as birds, fish, and the many other mysterious swimmers of whom we know little (representing the habitats of air, earth, and sea). It may seem like a time for preening but it is actually rather a moment to marvel that we as creatures share such a charge over our fellows. If we are honest we know that our responsibilities to birds, land-crawlers, and fish—the creatures that inhabit the realms above our heads and beneath our feet—are often exercised poorly and with but partial insight. Those animals, perhaps little known and surely not particularly well understood by us, have nonetheless been placed in our care.

With such assessments ringing in our ears—little people scarcely able to see the stars, struggling for speech, but made regent of the realm in which we dwell, flattered at the charge but humbled at its implications—we revisit the center of the psalm. As we, comparatively tiny, gaze up at the sun and moon that serve as reminders of our many human rhythms we marvel that God should remember and mark our human species, take note of us, graciously call us to mind. How do we see ourselves and how do we eye each other in view of God's persistent concern for us? As we stand at the heart of this figure that sizes us up we find that we cannot complacently notch our spot as big or little, important or fleeting, helpful or harmful, such is the complexity of the world in which we find ourselves. What we may be able to note—if not quite have the nerve to notch—is that our size is given, not scraped together by our hands. Our speech is ennobled by what we praise; our eyes are delighted by looking up at some mega-creatures, down at some mini-ones; our responsibilities are placed at our feet by their gracious artist; our deepest reflection is on the mystery of our remembrance and care in the heart of such a one.[3]

The challenge is to discern our status, to respond to what we learn as we slide this portion of the metaphor's edges together. We are valued, but why? If we shift back to our questions about our status, how important am I? how central? how right? how justified? how vulnerable? how deficient? We are uncertain, cannot quite peg ourselves—let alone the others. To cast blame and aspersion seems crude. To manufacture our own system of prizes or blame should, I think, strike us as ill-mannered. Comparisons are pointless except to redirect us back to the remembering and caring of God, except to recall to us that all that gives us status is a gift. Our simultaneous greatness and littleness, our paradoxically weak and powerful selves are the insight we are given here. We are interconnected with all else that is, not sovereign but responsible. The psalmist does not here mention any of our sinfulness, but perhaps the very omission of the topic reminds us that we have certain propensities to fall short of the glory within which we have been remembered and appointed.

What is our reaction to this picture of ourselves once we locate us at center stage with God, with God remembering us? Is it comforting? frightening? or both? Is it a view we find congenial or uncongenial? If we like it, why? if not, why? Does the lack of an absolute measure, the fact that we are not just big or small, centrally important or easily dismissible, disconcert or delight us? Our stature and status will to some extent have to remain at the threshold in any real assessment of human worth. The parable of Luke 15:11-32 poses some of the same issues for us. Though we may be accustomed to viewing it with strategies other than the spatial metaphor it works well with those once we have them in mind, thanks to the psalm. Let us look at it now and size up ourselves. Jesus begins: "'There was a man who had two sons. The younger of them said to his father, "Father, give me the share of the property that will belong to me." So he divided his property between them'" (Luke 15:11-12).

The parable opens with a quick introduction to the cast of characters, three different-sized people, a trio of individuals each with very distinctive stature and status. A father has two sons, one elder and one younger. The father, by attribution as well as by implication in this parable, begins honored, weighty, wealthy, prestigious. Though he seems to have no wife he has two sons and property. But his marks of status are no sooner noted than undermined when his son—and the younger one at that—demands a proleptic reading of the will. The boy's request for his share of the property is tantamount to wishing his father dead, acting as though he were dead. It is not only a personal affront to the father but a public shaming of him as well. To diminish an estate by whatever percentage now goes to the younger son is a public scandal in a small village, in a setting where every commodity is at a premium.

But as we listen to the story the father does not resist his son but accedes to his request for reasons that we do not hear but may speculate upon, with reactions we are not given but can undoubtedly understand. The father is minimized, shrunk not only by his younger son but by the silence of his elder one, who does not demur at his brother's request though his position should involve that responsibility. And the father in responding to the wish of his younger son, which may be the desire of the older boy as well, risks showing himself weak, reduced, vulnerable in our eyes as well as in the eyes of the village. Not only diminished, he is publicly humiliated and economically impoverished. The words "indulgent" and "permissive" may come to mind. The father may also seem weak, culpable, stupid. The fact that this paternal figure is often allegorized as God may tend to inhibit us from some of these negative judgments. But if we are reading parabolically rather than allegorically, identifying precisely who the father is may not be our main objective. We may not feel very sympathetic with any of the three at this point, and may decide that we are made of sterner stuff. Each character to some extent misuses his status and seems unworthy of it. But in any case, as Jesus resumes the narrative flow, their lives move along:

> "A few days later the younger son gathered all he had and traveled to a distant country, and there he squandered his property in dissolute living. When he had spent everything, a severe famine took place throughout that country, and he began to be in need. So he went and hired himself out to one of the citizens of that country, who sent him to his fields to feed the pigs. He would gladly have filled himself with the pods that the pigs were eating; and no one gave him anything. But when he came to himself he said, 'How many of my father's hired hands have bread enough and to spare, but here I am dying of hunger! I will get up and go to my father, and I will say to him, "Father, I have sinned against heaven and before you; I am no longer worthy to be called your son; treat me like one of your hired hands"'" (Luke 15:13-19).

The younger boy now gets a pair of scenes to himself, a narrative signaling of the very independence he was craving. Liquidating his new assets in some way, he severs his links with his father, brother, and home and transplants himself to a new country where his money enables him to live liberally. We are not given details but it seems unlikely that his wealth did not make him popular and give him a certain *cachet* among new acquaintances. He is a big man superimposed on being a little brother and a younger son. The status he has removed from his father he can, to some extent, add to his own persona. Undoubtedly he has fun, enjoys himself, attracts and includes others. But whatever advantage his inheritance lends him vanishes when his money goes. Whatever we may guess he and his new friends have done with it, the money is gone; we are told that even food now deserts him. Hiring out to care for pigs, the young Jewish boy finds his status suddenly and shockingly reduced. No longer ample, he is now deficient. After being independent and generous he suddenly becomes dependent, even envious of his porcine charges. He also, so far as human assistance is concerned, stands isolated, alone, friendless, powerless even to grab pig food. But having gone from son to owner to slave, he now plans his next shift in status.

What he does next we are fortunate to hear as he plans it. He takes out his pocket ruler, as it were, and assesses his stature—and not only his but those of others he knows. He says to himself, in effect, "I have less to eat than lots of people that work for my father at home; if I went home and asked for a job, asked to be put on the temporary or adjunct payroll, I could come close to what they have. My father has to hire someone and it may as well be me. I will ask for a job, show up on payday to get my wage. He will get some labor and I will get some money and food. The position of son is out for me, but the position of hired hand would fit me fine." He did not like his status as son, nor does he care for his state of being slave. Being rich he finds impermanent and he hopes being poor will end soon as well. If he cannot be popular at least he need not remain isolated. As he measures he takes an average: a "temporary," a "Kelly boy" is the solution he opts for. It is sensible, practical. Not everyone will agree with the paraphrase offered here, but before rejecting it, consider it in a bit more detail.

Before allowing us to hear the boy's soliloquy and subsequent to the information about his podless and starving condition Jesus, narrating the story, says, "'When he came to himself, he said . . . .'" What self does this boy have to come to? That he is hungry he knows; so he comes to his needy self rather than to his sated self. That is, as we have seen before when studying trees, a promising start. He also arguably comes to his spoiled son self, he the young man who asks and receives his share of the property with neither a paternal nor fraternal objection. I think it is safe, since the boy himself is measuring the stature of various actors in this drama, to do the same for him. What we are seeing so far is a boy who asks a share of livelihood outrageously and rudely from his father, receives it and wastes it, and now misses it. There is no thought of anyone except himself—which is not to say he does not mention others but simply to point out that he thinks of them only in reference to himself. The pigs might but do not help him get food; the owner is similarly useless. His father is an employer of others, and so presumably of himself now shortly. The hungry son does, to be sure, make a speech in which he acknowledges himself at fault before heaven and earth, sounding perhaps a bit like Psalm 8. And such an assessment is not easy to offer about oneself, especially to a superior, one diminished by us at that. The trouble with the speech is that the boy says it, rehearses it, and attaches to it a new demand. The speech is for himself really, rather than for his father. It is a campaign speech for a new promotion.

Again, since the boy is giving us his assessments we can go a bit farther and say that he continues to think of himself as central, as the one needing care, as one around whom plans must revolve. And he thinks of himself not exactly as dependent or independent, but as hired. He will neither owe nor be owed. He plans to work, to pick up his pay, to spend it as he likes—for food, clearly is what he is thinking. So he needs others to let him earn the things he wants. His measure of the man he calls his father is as boss. There is nothing filial in what he says, nor is there any sense in which the boy imagines that the man at home may be suffering, whether from poverty or something even more painful. Thin though this young man may be, he is still puffed up; needy, he remains a big man in his own estimation. Jesus continues the story:

> "So he set off and went to his father. But while he was still far off, his father saw him and was filled with compassion; he ran and put his arms around him and kissed him. Then the son said to him, 'Father, I have sinned against heaven and before you; I am no longer worthy to be called your son.' But the father said to his slaves, 'Quickly, bring out a robe—the best one—and put it on him; put a ring on his finger and sandals on his feet. And get the fatted calf and kill it, and let us eat and celebrate; for this son of mine was dead and is alive again; he was lost and is found!' And they began to celebrate" (Luke 15:20-24).

So it is such a boy who turns to go back the way he came, thinner, perhaps, than when he left home but in other ways rather much the same: spoiled, indulged, demanding, self-centered, lacking self-knowledge and awareness of his father. He may be continuing to rehearse his speech as he goes in order to get it just right and hone it to rhetorical persuasiveness. Since his part in the story is nearly over let me say that I do not think this a particularly negative portrait of him. I think it is a realistic one, even a hopeful one. Changing sizes is not easy. Big conversions can be famous but they are perhaps rare. That the younger son is headed home needy is a good start, but that he is still "a long way off," to stress Jesus' words, is pretty clear on more than one level; still, he is coming closer and about to be met. It may be close enough.

The father now comes back into the scene, or rather we rejoin him in the place he has not left. Unlike the boy who stands solely at the center of his own world, the father has been thinking of his younger son. How else does the father spot him when he is still a long way off? What do the neighbors think, how do they size up this old man as they glimpse him looking down the empty road? What is the father's self-appraisal as he continues to keep watch, to make rounds? It is difficult for me to think that he is much concerned about how he appears, about his status in others' eyes; he sees himself as the father of an absent son. And how does the father respond finally to the sight of the distant and distanced boy? He is moved with compassion, deeply stirred within. That is to say he suffers with his son, his own boundaries becoming increasingly permeable to the young man approaching him. That is what compassion means: an unchosen, unwilled, unavoidable giving over of some deep part of our self to another. As we look at the sizes of these two we see a contrast we may find helpful to contemplate.

As we are watching, narrative art imaging the boy physically larger as he draws near, we see the father lose some more dignity and status as he runs from the house to embrace the boy publicly, not at all worried about what his son may have in mind. The father also, quite visibly and audibly to the village, reinstates the boy as a son by clothing him, offering him what is probably the signet ring—equal to the credit card—and vesting the remaining property in him once again. The father, heedless of his own status, gives the boy access to the portion he has not already squandered. It is a tremendous act of confidence in the boy, perhaps a denying of what has in fact taken place, perhaps a vote of belief in the future. The actions make the compassion tangible: the father continues to give of his own life and livelihood to the son.

We again can see a number of possibilities in the behavior of the father. If the boy hopes to be able to have his brief discussion in private the father eliminates that option. If the boy worries about how the old man may receive him that concern is quickly ended as well. And despite all that happens around him—the compassionate greeting, the generous gift of clothing, the call for celebration—the boy begins on his calculated speech! Still thinking of his plan, he recites his first words. "'Father, . . . I . . . I . . . .'"

But then the father cuts in on him and for one reason or another does not allow him to finish. Perhaps he is not attending to his son's words, but perhaps the father is listening, knows exactly what is coming, and wishes to spare both of them the paltry shame of the boy's scenario. And the son stops. Again we need not idealize him since it will do us no good to pretend his size is other than it is. Inflating him will not help us size ourselves. Perhaps the boy cuts off his speech because he has already landed more than he contemplated getting for some time to come in his own plan; no need to wreck his position by asking for a wage when his gain has already surpassed his previous calculations. Or perhaps he is ashamed of his little scheme. It may be that he is genuinely reshaped now in the embrace of his father. Jesus, scarcely naïve about what is easy or difficult about resizing the self, does not decide for us when telling this story. Return, genuine conversion, is not easy, not accomplished by announcements, whether to ourselves or to others. Granted this boy has had the opportunity to learn a lot, and he may be ready to consolidate those experiences, but such a solution is far from certain in the parable. It is one of the places left for our filling in, perhaps variously on different occasions in our lives, as we read.

But the story goes on: "'Now his elder son was in the field; and when he came and approached the house, he heard music and dancing. He called one of the slaves and asked what was going on. He replied, "Your brother has come, and your father has killed the fatted calf, because he has got him back safe and sound." Then he became angry and refused to go in'" (Luke 15:25-28a).

The elder brother begins now to take shape more clearly before us, and for many readers of the story this is the character who wells up huge from inside. If we review the context in which the parable is set, the dismay of the righteous over the behavior of the unrighteous (Luke 15:1-2 and passim in chapters 9–19) we find that resonance is no accident. Such a discernment is never easy, for all that we often dismiss it in the gospels, as though the religious leaders—some of whom have to be sincere in their own efforts to understand what they need to do—should be able to figure out easily what Jesus is challenging them to rise to or become small enough to welcome it! So the big brother comes in from doing the work and finds the party already started. We might wave that detail away, decide that it is irrelevant or impertinent, as I have done myself, or see it as simply good storytelling: one scene wraps around the next so our interest does not flag.[4] But I think the master storyteller is not so heedless of the point. In a story about familial and public status and shame it is a most provocative detail. The celebration of the return of the wastrel, the handing over of more fattened goods to him for his enjoyment begins while the elder son is still doing the work on that very property— or at least on what remains of it! Not invited, he is not even informed and has to summon and quiz a servant to find out what is happening. It is an appalling moment for the older boy, a moment in which he can hardly avoid taking his own measure—and we take both his and ours in his shadow. For a storyteller, whose purpose is to share and prompt insight and deepening relationship, it is a superb stroke. The others, and the boy himself, have to confront something very painful about his stature.

We can measure with him as he will do shortly in our hearing: he is reliable, responsible, capable, obedient, right about many things. He is caught by the sound of the music, which has to sound in his ears as a terrible betrayal of himself once he understands what occasions it. Like his father who is moved profoundly, far below the level of choice, so is this son. Angry, he refuses to go in. He takes his stance outside, proud and refusing to bend, again making a public statement of his lack of solidarity with both father and brother. His refusal to act as host marks the family as still split, brings all of them under the scrutiny of the interested neighbor-guests. His anger makes this son heedless of the dishonor he is bringing once again on his father and on himself.

> "His father came out and began to plead with him. But he answered his father, 'Listen! For all these years I have been working like a slave for you, and I have never disobeyed your command; yet you have never given me even a young goat so that I might celebrate with my friends. But when this son of yours came back, who has devoured your property with prostitutes, you killed the fatted calf for him!' Then the father said to him, 'Son, you are always with me, and all that is mine is yours. But we had to celebrate and rejoice, because this brother of yours was dead and has come to life; he was lost and has been found'" (Luke 15:28b-32).

The father, getting smaller as he faces without denial the deficiencies of his elder son as well as his younger son and as he copes publicly with his own clear inadequacy as a father, goes outside once again to meet a child, goes with compassion. Jesus does not use the word again but once we have understood it as a matter of porous boundaries of the self and a rush to enclose another with love, then of course we recognize it when we see it again so soon. There is no false dignity here, no trying to pretend that the embarrassing breach is not occurring. The father does not try to allege something that all will know not to be so, to rise above a situation that shows his own radical insufficiency. Nor does he resolve privately to deal with the absent son later, or to point out to the assembled guests how rudely and provocatively the elder boy is behaving. With either of those responses he would be gathering his own edges tightly into place, preserving his own sovereign skin against another whose behavior would invade it.

We see here one of the clearest differences between reading allegory and reading parable. Labeling the father allegorically we can indeed conclude, as is traditional, that he stands for God. Then the comments about his shrinking stature do not fit and must be dismissed as facets of the narrative figure that have to be discarded. On the other hand if we are engaging the figure parabolically, catching the ways in which the rising and falling sizes of all three of these figures show us our own status, then the vulnerability of the father and even his apparent unfairness become central. He may show us the depths of the heart of God without our needing to label him as a cipher for God. Let us reflect on what he does and says.

First he allows and listens to an address from the angry boy that sounds rude even to our ears, which are arguably less sensitive than those of the audience for whom Jesus first tells the story. There is no filial address to the father, no courtesy title. "'Listen!'" he accuses, demands. Then the boy shapes his narrative to cast his father as a boss, a strict taskmaster, while picturing himself as an obedient and long-suffering slave denied even the wage of an unfatted goat as a pretext for gathering his friends around him. By contrast, he accuses, when a disobedient and prodigal "son of yours" returns the father kills the fatted calf for him.

Before hearing the father's response we can note a few more things about how the boy describes himself. If we are alert we will have the sense that we have heard it before, as indeed we have. For the older son's charge is close in attitude to the younger son's rehearsed speech. Each of them thinks of the male parent as primarily an owner of property, even as one standing between the goods and each boy's desire to share them more fully. Each son thinks of his father as a source of stuff. And perhaps that is so. The elder son speaks longingly, if angrily, of festivities of which he is deprived, imagining revels that his brother can recall— telling us details we did not witness in the narrative portion of the parable though we may have imagined them too. The elder son also betrays, now if not before, that he too has been eyeing the goods and wishing to wrest some of them from his father. Unlike his brother, he does not ask; but now he is blaming his father for failing to give him even a small share of what he clearly feels is his due; he criticizes his parent for squandering even more of the property on "'this son of yours,'" of killing the fatted calf "'for him.'" Sizes? Like the psalm, the parable shows us a paradoxical image. These two brothers are very much alike, displeasing though that would undoubtedly be to both and hidden though it is likely to remain from them. It is a truism that we project what is uncomfortable for us onto the scorecards of others. Jesus gives in story form a vivid example of ourselves performing precisely that assessment but offers us as well the chance to see it clearly.

The father, having patiently admitted this barrage of rudeness from his angry son, addresses him courteously as well as lovingly. "'Son,'" he calls him, though we have never heard this boy call his parent "father." And what he says is instructive. "'All that is mine is yours,'" he explains. The boys—both sons—misunderstand that relationship from the start. We are told that the father divides his substance between them: which of them? Do the demanding brother and the remaining estate split the goods? the two brothers? It is not clear. But the father implies that is not so much the point. To the boy's charge that the father has never given him a single goat the father replies that all the goats are already his, and more. "'You are with me,'" he explains. The "yours" and "mine" is an "our," he clarifies, making the boundaries porous and the status unclassifiable once again. So the father's first point again helps us assess stature. The boy feels impoverished, isolated, and deprived; the father says what we share is plenty. The shock of the two speeches is the difference between them. How can this boy, how can both sons know this spacious father so little? How can the elder son labor with his father all those years, as he tells us he has done, and fail to know that in his father's view all the goods are shared? How can the younger son imagine that the one awaiting his return home will consent to hire him as a temp? It is a sobering pair of questions. It is the same assessment made very independently by the brothers in isolation from each other. Seeing the poverty of the father is part of the insight offered from the parable.

The father's second point is perhaps the very thing we need to hear from him. He explains, in effect, that the feast is not simply for the prodigal: "'. . . it is necessary that we celebrate. . . .'" There is no clear distinction between himself and his sons, between the fatted calf freely shared round and the goat of which the boy feels so deprived. The father explains, as he consistently shows in his actions, that the separations among the three are false. He makes important to his older son that he is with his father; he explains that they must celebrate the return of the younger as well. The father sees not two isolated boys squabbling across him for possessions, but his sons whom he loves despite their shortcomings. He invites each of his sons to see father and brother as more than just people to be got around or to compete with. The parable does not deny the feelings and fear of unfairness, the worry most of us nourish that somehow we will be deprived of what is ours, that we will be demeaned in some fundamental way. Rather, in a very honest way the story that Jesus tells invites us to stand within this welter of measurements, to participate and look compassionately at ourselves and at each other—even at God, who we may think also falls short on occasion!

And once again we see a parable that seems cut off prematurely, stops rather than finishes. How will the younger son do once he has a signet ring to manage? How will the older son do now that he has been encouraged to think of the goats and fatted calves as his own? Will the father change his permissive responses to try and get the sons back into line? The ending of the parable lies not with them but more with ourselves. Jesus, journeying to Jerusalem with a mixed crew of younger and elder offspring, with his brothers and sisters, is unlikely to be complacent about happy endings.

Depending on what we have seen here, as we watch these figures we may have new insight about our size and status. Like Psalm 8 the narrative does not let us quite secure a place, does not encourage us to decide that one size will fit us for all time. Big or small, important or insignificant, isolated or related, coherent or conflicted, receiving or earning: we spend some time in all of these places and may hope that someone is watching for our return, no matter where we may be. We think about God thinking about us.

NOTES: CHAPTER 3

[1]A thorough and excellent discussion of the impact of the physical arrangement of language on our reading selves can be found in Phyllis Trible's *Rhetorical Criticism: Context, Method, and the Book of Jonah* (Minneapolis: Fortress, 1994). Such artistic arrangements, often called structures, are highly nuanced in their capacities for communicating.

[2]Without delving into detail about the specific social markers about the authors or presumed speakers of the psalms I will tend to balance the gender roles between the figures in the parable and the psalm. Since in the present essay the parable concerns a father and two sons I will reference the psalmist as female.

[3]The two Hebrew verbs translated here as "remember" and "care for" are rich. The verb "remember/*zkr*" does not imply that God has first forgotten but rather suggests freshly focused attention. The second, *pqd*, has a range of meanings including "to muster, appoint, visit," suggesting again our status as both recipients and agents.

[4]This insight, more clearly than some others that are undoubtedly gained from the teaching of parables, comes from a student, Javier Zavala, who argued it in such a way that it overcame my initial resistance to it. Himself both a son and a father, he found the father's action painful here.

4

Searching Faces:
Psalm 27 and Luke 18:9-18

*T*o scan faces that we encounter is an almost continuous experience in the ordinary days most of us spend. We catch the
glances and expressions of those we know best, anticipating
what we find with pleasure or dread; is it a good time to ask a favor, tell
of a disaster, make a point, or not? We scrutinize the faces of beloved
older or sick friends for some sign of improvement or to assure ourselves
there is no deterioration. We read the facades of people we do not know
and imagine what has produced such visages. We often think we can see
quite a lot, perhaps in a kind old face or in a dissipated one, or that we can
read a frittered life in the spoiled and discontented face greeting us from
the magazine rack at the supermarket checkout stand. There is much to
see, for all that remains hidden. And perhaps we are right in what we
conclude, at least on many occasions. All the while we are reading them,
others are reading us as well, seeing things of which we may have little
idea, however familiar our faces may feel to us who live behind them. As
we search the many faces presented to us in a day, in a phase of our life,
in our whole span, what are we searching for as we watch other seekers?

The metaphoric entry we will use for Psalm 27 and Luke 18:9-18 is
more complex than the last two we have explored and works in a
slightly different way. When we consider the lives of two trees in relationship to our own selves we find many ways in which their processes
well describe our own. We discover perhaps that the rooted tree has
more practical secrets to share with us than we may at first think. And

as we explore the realities of our own measurable sizes, struggling for a stable sense of ourselves in relation to something else, we discover ourselves tall in certain modes, tiny in others, arrogant or humble by turns, competently in control of some situations but quite klutzy in others. We watch two sons draw themselves up to full stature but look quite inadequate while we observe their father, constantly diminished, refusing to rely on a false status or dignity he might be able to clutch if he did not continue to stand in relation to his two sons.

The searching face is closer to the workings of status than it is to the tree since it is metonymic as well as metaphoric. That is, our faces, being part of our bodies, can stand for the whole of us, and they usually show forth our most communicative aspect. When our forehead wrinkles, an eyebrow lifts, our eyes melt, our nostrils flare, our mouths relax, we are offering a great deal about ourselves. Thus as we read a face we take the part as typically expressive or indicative of the totality. Though I will make use of that trope I am more interested in the metaphoric sense of the several faces in these texts offering us sets of experience to help us better understand our own. In that sense the faces are like costumes we can try on and wear for a while in order to come to deeper awareness that we have to some extent already lived each particular role for which we have a face offered us. To put that same point slightly differently: the expressive and desiring faces we will search are like people in a police lineup, lounging or cringing in some aspect against a wall, unable to see us as we stare at them; we, sitting in presumed safety behind an one-way glass, suddenly spot ourselves where we may little have expected to do so and rise, uncertain, to our feet in anxiety but also in new insight. The juxtaposition of these variedly expectant faces next to our own domesticated surfaces can redraw our experience in fresh ways. It is, then, in the sense of the costume or the lineup that we can begin working with our metaphor of searching faces. We have five to try on for size. Let us begin with the psalm, though this time visiting both Old and New Testament texts by turns.

1 The Lord is my saving light;
whom should I fear?
God is my fortress;
what should I dread?
2 When the violent come at me
to eat me alive,
a mob eager to kill—
they waver, they collapse.

3 Should battalions lay siege,
  I will not fear;
  should war rage against me,
  even then I will trust.
4 One thing I ask the Lord,
  one thing I seek;
  to live in the house of God
      every day of my life;
  caught up in God's beauty,
  at prayer in the temple.
5 The Lord will hide me there,
  hide my life from attack—
  a sheltering tent above me,
  a firm rock below.
6 I am now beyond reach
      of those who besiege me.
  In the temple I will offer
      a joyful sacrifice;
  I will play and sing to God.

As we stand with the psalmist gazing out from her home, what do we see? the violent coming into the neighborhood, the mob setting up camp outside the house. As she sees these preparations, the arraying of forces for siege, and as she scans the faces of the opponents she and we can too vividly imagine the fierce encounter that lies ahead. Threats to our life, to our adequacy surround us. The imagery of warfare need not evoke a literal "Desert Storm" scenario but rather any situation where we are surrounded by danger to our self, to our well being, to what we treasure and value. What do we hear her say under such circumstances? "No problem! Whom should I fear? What shall I dread? I will not fear! Still do I trust." It may sound like whistling in the dark—our brave words lined up and put through maneuvers to reassure us who command them—or it can seem a boast of the rashly self-confident. I think here it can also be a prayer for security, a prayer to God who can provide us with some sort of antidote to our fears. Our first face, then, is the psalmist's, threatened and responding in confidence to God—which is surely not the inevitable choice! Knowing what she has seen (threats roundabout) and what she has said ("I count on God") what comes next? Having searched out the advancing danger this woman of faith speaks serenely and simultaneously scurries closer to security. Let us accompany her, since this journey is surely familiar to us.

The security sought is that which God provides: as envisioned here the refuge is Zion, the rock, Jerusalem, the mountain, the tent, the Temple, its liturgy. The refuge for us is a lavishly layered place, itself a metaphor for the embrace of God. Zion is the name given to the cosmic mountain where God dwells, its ancient roots going deep into the heart of the earth, its crest brushing highest heaven. As does the city Jerusalem, God's chosen place of encounter with the lives of worshipers rests on rock. We, fleeing what threatens us in company with the householder of this prayer, our faces reflecting anxiety, arrive to be guest-dwellers in God's space, are swept gladly into the liturgy that rises there joyously, continuously, solid and secure. Danger drives us deeper into God's embrace and worry makes room for worship. So far, so good!

Jesus starts us out with a similar scenario, stripped of details we have no trouble resupplying as he no doubt expects we shall do. "He also told this parable. . . .[1] 'Two men went up to the temple to pray, one a Pharisee and the other a tax collector'" (Luke 18:9-10). We need first to stop and be sure we know the outlines of who these two figures are and then to fill them in a bit from our own experience. Familiar to us though their tags will be—once we hear "Pharisee and tax collector" we think we have already "done" them—we need to slow down and look more carefully. What do we see in the faces of these two who, shoulder to shoulder, enter the rock, Zion, Jerusalem, the Temple, privileged place of access to God?

Both are Jewish men. The tax collector (or publican) is a petty functionary of the Roman imperial presence in Judea. His job would have been something like that of a toll collector on a bridge or highway of our experience, taking from all passersby the money required to pay for the "service" provided by headquarters. Adequately-maintained roads are a convenience for an indigenous population but local comfort is scarcely the reason that occupying powers keep them in good repair. So to take tolls is to collaborate with oppressors. The collecting of goods worked slightly differently in Roman Judea than it may in our town or state, but the general process is readily imaginable by us. It is not a job of prestige; in fact to relieve people of their money in order to pay for the services of the oppressor presence, perhaps additionally to line one's own pockets even a little, is conspicuously devoid of status. So as we ponder the face of this man we see nothing arrogant, perhaps rather some shame or some quiet defiance since he is supporting his family as best he can do. He may be somewhat dishonest, though he need not be. Perhaps we do not know for certain, even if we suspect that he may on occasion exact something extra if he thinks it can be done.

The man who enters the Temple with him looks much like him. He, too, is a layman, a man with responsibilities toward those he loves. His clothing may be slightly less workaday; he may exhibit the traditional marks of an observant Jew. His face is eager rather than serious and he seems comfortable as he moves quickly among the others who are there that day near the hour for public prayer. If we are looking for him among our own acquaintances the closest analogue may be the permanent lay deacon: a man who has a family and a job but who has made room as well for some special observances and for service to other lay people. Such a man is not far from an equivalent of what a Pharisee would have been at the time of Jesus.[2]

A particular problem meets us here as we scrutinize the faces of these two, and it is not simply a "Bible problem." The generic lineaments that are likely to emerge every time we hear "Pharisee and publican" are so set that it is difficult to look at their actual, idiosyncratic behaviors. For reasons rising from our familiarity with Scripture we tend to decide too quickly what these two stand for: the Pharisee is a smug hypocrite, the publican a benign and lionized rip-off agent. When we see certain faces we may do the same thing: all poor dirty people are liable to want to grab our belongings; my friend who always turns every situation into a complaint about her job will only do it again, no matter what words I offer her. The challenge is to see beyond what seems likely, what we have learned to expect, to something a little fresher. The two men whose faces we scrutinize as they go by us into the Temple to do whatever we will watch them do are people like us: predictable to some extent, but more fundamentally individual, the way we are or want to be and hope people will bother to expect from us. Familiar, certainly they are, but well worth our continued observation. They may—in fact must—surprise us.

Sometimes when working on this parable with college students, who share to some extent our problem of familiarity with many of these classic images from Scripture (for even if they do not understand the texts particularly deeply they have heard them preached frequently) I reset the scenario to get their attention. A student-customized introduction begins: "Two students went up to the teacher after the midterm bluebooks had been handed back. One approached defiantly, scalp shaven and tattooed, features pierced and ringed, carrying a motorcycle helmet; the other strode forward, freshly preppy in L. L. Bean informal togs, smoothing fluffy hair, its tints visible under the classroom's fluorescent lights, off a furrowed brow. One of them had gotten an A–, the other a C+." Before even hearing more of the story students can readily imagine what several kinds of things might be about to unfold, and more important, they can envision themselves in either pair of shoes, behind either face, underneath either scalp. Though the details of the characters' dress and demeanor are not without relevance those features need to be coordinated with and may even give way before something else. The boring, polarized, predictable stereotype is suddenly freshly presented for negotiation.

My students stir in their chairs, lean forward, shuffle their feet— classic nonverbal sign of student engagement. They recognize at once, intuitively, that the two "uniforms" cover up something more vital and urgent. And these bluebook-familiars sitting as audience before me can themselves begin to imagine a whole theater of faces receiving back exams rather than just the two most obvious ones: happy faces, satisfied ones, proud ones, angry or crushed or worried faces, tear-stained ones, blank and self-protecting visages. And behind any of these faces is not simply a stereotype but a fresh human experience. We need to be able to sketch out a similar sort of scene for our face-watching selves, one that we cannot predict before we hear more.[3]

So as we look at the faces of the people approaching the Temple at Jerusalem, at least so far the beleaguered person from Psalm 27 and the two men from the parable, we recognize that they bring with them—or we carry with us—our issues of fairness, some concern for the viability of hard-won achievements, our "I'd never do that" banners; we bring with us our fear of failure and of loss of face, our entitlements, our plaques and awards. Not simply tourists stopping off at God's dwelling, we come carrying with us the things for which we want credit and approval, esteem and satisfaction, and we bring our worries and deficiencies, hoping to trade them in or get them retreaded in some way. If we are like most people I know we will be wondering a bit about the others: the ones who are setting up the siege apparatus outside my home, the ones from whom I have collected tolls (and will again), the ones with whom I work in the believing community. Henri Nouwen was fond of an image that remains vivid for me: a huge scoreboard like those visible in sports arenas is what we lug around with us to every encounter we have, hoping that we and the universe will be able to keep track of how effectively we are trouncing our opponent who is everyone else. So as we look at and behind these three faces of ourselves seeking security we may be able to see an array of possibilities, not simply the most obvious that we can easily disclaim.

As we begin to listen as well as look, what do we hear? Jesus continues,

"The Pharisee, standing by himself, was praying thus, 'God, I thank you that I am not like other people: thieves, rogues, adulterers, or even like this tax collector. I fast twice a week; I give a tenth of all my income.' But the tax collector, standing far off, would not even look up to heaven, but was beating his breast and saying, 'God, be merciful to me, a sinner!'" (Luke 18:11-13).

So what we hear and see now gives us additional insight into their faces, into our own faces.[4] We search their faces, seeking in some way, as are they, for security.

The Pharisee, as we have already observed, is a devout layman to whom a relationship with God and community is very important. His prayer, which we are able to overhear as he utters it, is perhaps mirrored in his face and his general demeanor. He is standing to pray as is customary, his face turned up to the heavens, his eyes closed. Since he, standing, is prominent, we can see his face as we hear his words. His speech is truthful, his sentiments religious. He begins by thanking God, a promising overture to any prayer. We may read some joy or satisfaction in his face, some particular reason he has come to the holiest place of Judaism at a time of public prayer in order to address God. We may appreciate that there are times when a simple, informal expression of gratitude or acknowledgment of a favor seems inadequate to a situation. We are eager to make our response more formal. One reason for our reading this man's face, and our own, is to contemplate reasons that have brought him into God's house to pray.

As his lips continue to move the Pharisee enumerates deeds he has truly done, practices in fact he is committed to do in the future and will undoubtedly accomplish. He fasts not only when he is obligated to do so—once a year—but at other times as well; in fact he counts them up: twice a week. He tithes generously, not grudging or trying to avoid his responsibilities by exempting any of his goods. Again we may find, prompted by the Pharisee's clear example, that no small portion of our own prayer is turning over with God, in God's presence, the things that we do, things we perhaps struggle to accomplish and are grateful when we have managed with God's help to secure them, to make them a part of our regular lives. The man standing here in prayer is making such a statement. We are with him so far and can most likely recognize ourselves in the surface of his features without too much of a stretch.

But of course between thanking God and mentioning what he is grateful for this man has made some other announcements as well.

Here, since it is his face we are watching, we see him open his eyes and cast them about the area where he is standing, perhaps in hopes of additional inspiration. And since his gaze moves out to search out others he includes them in his prayer: "thieves, rogues, adulterers." We wonder if he sees colleagues of his own, scoundrels who have defrauded him; but how does he know who has committed adultery? Perhaps his certainty begins to make us uneasy. If he does not know that some of those standing also at prayer are in fact thieves, rogues, and adulterers, why and on what basis does he assume that they are?

If we have tried to slow ourselves down a bit from stereotyping this man too quickly just because we think we know what his label signifies or have heard him too glibly dismissed on many occasions, then we are more sensitized when he does the very same thing to the people he sees. As he looks around he categorizes quickly those who are caught into his sweep, and we must wonder: based on what information? What does he see in their faces that helps him assign these tags to them? But let us suppose, in our effort to be as generous as possible, that in fact on that day some thieves and rogues and adulterers have shown up to pray as well—since we know in fact that at least one ne'er-do-well is on site. When the Pharisee gives thanks that he is not even like "this tax collector" we know he is on firm ground at least in his identification. The toll-taker may well be known to the Pharisee, so in this case at least his label is correct.

But even before he gets to his own good deeds, and prior to his slotting of the others, he has already compromised his prayer of thanks by an even more damning remark. What can he mean when he, looking around God's dwelling at the rest of God's children, is grateful that he sees no one like himself, himself like no one there? How is he so sure that he does not resemble any that he sees? And why, even if such a thing might be so, is it good news to him? Having started by thanking God, this man betrays too quickly that it is himself he is really congratulating. Naming God once, he refers to himself repeatedly. Addressing God, he really announces to himself that he is doing very well to be unlike the others. But to give him as much credit as we can do—especially if we are beginning to be reminded of ourselves by his demeanor and prayer—suppose he is really not like them in a number of ways. Perhaps he really does not steal, is not a rogue, has not committed adultery. What is wrong in his saying so?

Beside his too-confident labeling and his arrogant selection of categories stands his assumption that he can know what data are important to read for as he scans and what can be disregarded. How does he know that the deeds he enumerates are better than the ones he gives thanks for having avoided? Well, we may find it obvious in the ethical system of Judaism and Christianity that the deeds he celebrates—fasting, tithing—are commanded and commended; those he pulls his skirts away from—theft, adultery—are proscribed. So where is the problem?

Let us look at him, his face, again. Is his face, his assessment smug or compassionate? Is he concerned about the others and recognizing a near-miss for himself? Is he willing to walk over to the others to see how he can help his friends or eager to avoid them altogether? Where is he standing: off by himself verbally, emotionally, spiritually, if not physically? His words have made clear his prayer posture: he begins by concluding with pride that he is not like the rest of the human community, not in need of anything from God. And as our earnest layman addresses God is his assumption that God is congratulating him as well, agreeing with his self-assessment and appraisal of the others? If prayer is a pouring out of our needy selves in search of a response from God, is there anything needy about this man? It is difficult to hear that he is asking for anything—even approval! Or to put it slightly differently: if what he searches for is approval, credit, esteem, gratitude, admiration, on what basis is his quest? How will those help him? He seems confident that he has achieved all that is needed. Nor does he seem conscious that the pinnacle on which he is standing may be perilous, slippery. We listen in vain for any awareness that the gap between tithing and thieving is sometimes tiny. How Jesus clothes and labels him—shaved head or fluffy tresses—is less important than our reading his appeal.

So his journey to the dwelling of God, his face raised up in the holy place, is not because he recognizes some need for God's secure rock. We can appreciate, I think, that though the psalmist's words and those of this Temple-goer can sound rather similar ("whom should I fear? . . . what should I dread? . . . I will not fear . . . I will trust . . .; I give you thanks that I am not . . . I fast . . . I tithe . . .") the difference is between asking for and relying on something outside our own grasp and feeling confident that everything is under our control. The psalmist, worried, comes to seek something, but the Pharisee already has it all, knows it all. The faces of those two are very different as they turn to God, even as they look out upon the other.

If the Pharisee and those looking closely and recognizing him were to arrange props for the scene we might provide a mirror and a microphone so that we can watch our own performance and be sure that all who need to hear it can get the good word. In our quest for the security of virtue, the desire for visibility is high. In a sense that is good news, since once we recognize what we are doing it will be too blatant to deny. Jesus talks about "the Pharisee" a lot while journeying to Jerusalem, and it is going to be difficult to shut this face out of our inquiries. As Jesus seems to have done, we may encounter this face several times each day.

And since the Pharisee has called our attention to the toll collector we can take a longer look at him. He, as Jesus describes him for us, stands apart—so also in some way by himself, isolated, lonely, alone. He is not looking around at the others; whatever he is seeking he does not need to scan to find it. His face is difficult to see directly since this man is a bit hunched, beating his breast in a feeling of emotion and deep sorrow expressed in a common ritual gesture. He is mumbling or whispering, harder to hear than the other. But since he repeats the same expression continuously we can finally catch his words. He, like the other, addresses God bluntly and directly—no titles or formal address to buffer. "God, be merciful to me, a sinner" (Luke 18:13). There is no comparison by this man with any other though Jesus in describing the scene for us is making the contrast clear.

The man assesses himself and finds that he is a sinner, undifferentiated but clear. It is impossible and unimportant to guess what particulars lie under the general blanket of his single word "sinner." It may be toll collectors' sins of greed, theft, envy, financial mismanagement, sociopolitical complicity. It is plausible that he is a rogue and adulterer as has been suggested. The special tithings of everything he owns and the optional fasts are not his responsibility since unlike the Pharisee he has not taken them on as an obligation, nor are they sins were they to be omitted. I think we may understand that whatever the tax collector is referencing to himself—and to God—as he prays, it is not minor. He is not a petty sinner pretending to a big role. There is something, whether one crime or some repeated failing, keenly felt, admitted, grieved over, still clutched, perhaps not quite shaken off. That he does not specify his sins in our hearing does not mean he is not admitting them. His word is blunt and unmistakable if conveniently generic, so that we can step in without a problem. The fact that he is so often appraised positively when compared to his prayer partner need not blind or deafen us to what he is expressing.

So like the other he addresses God and then talks about himself. But unlike the other he makes no comparisons or contrasts and he asks for something rather than listing his contributions. Searching the face of God he asks, begs, for mercy, which according to Jesus is a highly appropriate thing to seek from God. Mercy, as we recall in the characters of the intervening gardener and the forgiving father, is gratuitous: undeserved, not to be presumed upon, intangible, uncontrollable, nonentitled. Confidence is not the same as presumption. This man asks for a gift he has no claim upon. It is even conceivable that he will need to ask again, may not be able quite to harness the gift of grace he begs to receive.

To ask God for mercy and to go over one's own accounts in God's supposed ledger are two very different appraisals not only of self but of God. How each of these persons at prayer reads the visage of God is instructive for us as we conduct our own search. How we read God's attentive face is key as well. Is God best pleased when we make mention of all that we have done for God or when we recall all that God may do for us? The polarity is probably misleading but again it makes the contrast stark. As these two approach their encounter with the face of God, the one looking around, the other down, who sees best? How do our faces, so like those we have been watching, seek out the face of God?

Before rejoining that question in the company of the psalmist whom we left at the rock sanctuary of God, we can observe one other thing about these two men. Suppose that in addition to these two whom Jesus has just drawn for us in the Temple that day there is another visitor whose face we glimpse, a woman whom Luke will in fact place there in just three more chapters.[5] This woman, who is poor, her purse and savings soon to be depleted as she puts her last two coins into the Temple treasury, may stand not so far from the two men, in prayer herself. Let us position her somewhere between these other two so that she is able to overhear them as well as we have done.

One of them she recognizes as her "lay deacon," prone to urge her by his example and word to make her life as holy and pleasing to God as possible. He may even encourage her from time to time to contribute funds to some special and worthy project of his. The other man, whom she recognizes as well, also occasionally relieves her of a bit of money in order to assist her to meet her obligations to the occupying power. Each of them is from her angle a sort of tough overseer of her good and goods, perhaps neither particularly esteemed by her. She may react to them both the way we do to groups who send us pleading letters and return envelopes; whether the cause be a political reelection campaign, the poor children of Tijuana, or a no-lose sweepstakes, we may have a common and unnuanced reaction. The value of thinking about these two from the perspective of a third party is once again to shake them free from the calcification we may have placed around them, where the one is all good, the other all bad. The widow at prayer also reminds us that we are most likely neither one nor the other of "the men" but careen between the two, can identify with both of them, resemble the pair of them both to ourselves and to others watching and reading our faces. Neither of them might be pleased to be mistaken for the other, nor are we happy to be credited with deeds that we pride ourselves on not doing. But so it is. Like the two sons of the father in Luke 15, each undoubtedly aware of profound differences between himself and the other, these two men may look quite alike to those searching their faces with a different experience or hope.

As we turn back to the psalmist, our first "face" who has taken refuge in the Temple, what are we observing? The last we heard she was rejoicing in the festive liturgy, feeling secure in the rock. But somehow as we were occupied with the characters in the parable she has seen or been shown a deeper level. As we listen in again as she prays we go as well to a new phase with her. She begs:

7 O God, listen to me;
   be gracious, answer me.
8 Deep within me a voice says,
   "Look for the face of God!"
   So I look for your face;
9 I beg you not to hide.
   Do not shut me out in anger,
   help me instead.
   Do not abandon or desert me,
   my savior, my God.
10 If my parents rejected me,
   still God would take me in.
11 Teach me how to live;
   lead me on the right road
   away from my enemies.
12 Do not leave me to their malice;
   liars breathing violence
      rise to swear against me.
13 I know I will see
      how good God is
   while I am still alive.
14 Trust in the Lord. Be strong.
   Be brave. Trust in the Lord.

Her cry of joy (v. 6) has, as is inevitable, given way to a place of diminished or faltering serenity. We watch her face as she now pleads with God: "I cry out, listen! Answer, be merciful. My heart reminds you of what you told me: 'Seek my face!' So now do not hide from me or push me away—or walk away from me. Gather me, teach me, lead me" (vv. 8-9). We wonder, recognizing her desperation lest she lose what she has just experienced, how the change in demeanor came about? Recently secure in our refuge, how are we undermined so quickly? As in the parable we have a pair of alternates, if not opposites, coming to search from diverse experiences. Where is the place where we feel we can set a foot firmly, in which we can feel secure? How do we secure access to God's face? How hard do we try? Do we try?

The psalmist shows us again perhaps a face between those of the Pharisee and the toll collector: neither arrogant nor depressed, neither heedless of sin nor obsessed by it. Or better, here we can discern the facets that compose the other two and reexamine them once more, bringing them even closer to ourselves. Which face of God do we seek: the accounting side or the gift-giving side? What presence do we long to share: the one who owes us or the one in whose debt we already are happily plunged? The psalmist says, in a verse that is difficult in Hebrew,[6] that her heart prompts her, or prompts God, in the relationship: "My heart reminds 'us' to mention this again!" Whose reminding heart do we see animating the faces of the two men at prayer in the parable?

Why does God's face vanish, or seem to? What is our reaction when it goes, or seems absent? Do we miss it, follow it, call out for it? or not? God's face is our good, our security; it is all goodness that we want and cannot accomplish, are unable to secure under our own steam. It is our refuge from "the others," those camping outside our house, whoever they are; it can console us even when we are let down by those like our parents on whose love we should be able to count. The psalmist says here that such opponents have followed her even into God's house, have undermined the confidence she felt, her toes resting on that cosmic rock. If our opponents were all clearly very bad it might be easier to cope with them; since some of them sit next to us in the pew it becomes more challenging. Our non-well-wishers can follow us right in to access to God and can threaten by their presence to cut off the very security to which we might feel entitled! It is a valuable clue, this feeling of entitlement.

The psalmist ends her prayer as she began it, or at least the words are similar. "Trust . . . be strong . . . be brave . . . trust in the Lord"

(vv. 1-3, 14). But she has been through a lot since she uttered these words in the early verses of the psalm. She cannot corner God irretrievably, cannot eliminate the sense of losing God's face for the moment. But she knows she can continue to seek it, to ask for the mercy of it. The face that is disturbed, restless, worried can become serene, confident, hopeful. The eyes in such a face can look on others as similar rather than as threats. As she leaves the Temple and returns to her besieged home to take up the threads of her life again it may not be so very different, but she is. And when things grow frightening again—maybe even before they do!—she will flee back to God's face.

The parable, we may note, is not quite so satisfactorily finished. As the two Jewish men leave the Temple on this occasion Jesus remarks that one is justified rather than the other, just as we anticipate while watching them. But that sentence does not tell us as much as we may wish to know. What does each man leave to do? What do their eyes search out as they walk past us on their way out? Do they see each other again? If the toll collector goes home justified, which is what Jesus reads in his searching of the human condition, what is it that he has read? If the Pharisee will need to come again, perhaps in a different mode or mood, how will that occur?

What about the woman of Luke 19 who has seen her "deacon" and her "taxman" in the Temple that day? Compared with the few pennies she still has in her purse their accounts are no doubt substantial, their lives more secure than hers. Each is better off by far than she in the world they all inhabit. The worries she takes with her as she leaves the Temple, that she takes to bed each night and that greet her the following morning, are not the ones of which they are speaking so earnestly, each in his own way. So while at the same time we recognize the differences between them, which are indeed easily observable, we simultaneously recall that what seems stark by one measure is scarcely distinguishable from another angle. Might such an insight help the Pharisee see himself as pompous, the publican catch his own assessment as overwrought? As we may recall from trying to stabilize our status, the inability to position it firmly may help us to take it less seriously. The widow's prayer to God, we may imagine, is to keep her dwindling goods out of the grasp of both of these takers! When she eventually drops her last coins into the Temple treasury they are at least saved from the hands of these two. But who will see to her security?

Having spent considerable time searching out the depths and possibilities of these five intense faces let us sum up our inquiry: we have allowed the psalmist two faces—first, threatened but gaining security; next, secure in God's presence but sensing it threatened as well. The lay religious leader was seeking little that he had not already engineered himself; the toll collector was perhaps spending too much time on seeking the wrong things and sensing that he might be missing something key. And we hypothesized a widow, wordlessly pondering her priorities, thinking about the investment of her last coins. If this is our set of possible suspects, what is our assessment as we peer eagerly through the glass that seems to separate us from them? How do we sort what fits from what does not?

So much does fit that we need not linger too much with that part of the metaphor process. Those who feel beleaguered and seek refuge in something other than retaliation, who cry out to and for what they fear is receding, who count up their good deeds with God's arm around them, who bring their deficiencies to that circle as well, offering their hard-earned experience for assessment while God listens: these are characters with whom we hope to stand, faces in whose company we long to be. The search may tempt us—certainly it tempts me—to accept the three women at prayer and deny the two men. After all, I can thank God that I am neither a totally dispirited sinner who can scarcely muster the words to amend a life nor a smug superstar, feeling totally outside the human condition. But that would be too fast a move. The fact that we choose to see the psalmist at two sides of her prayer and draw the widow identifying as similar the two men in the Temple provides, perhaps, our cue to what is semantically dissonant in this transaction.

As soon as I thank God that I am like the psalmist and unlike the Pharisee the same alarm needs to go off at my words that I have heard so well and so often when I watch him. Who is "the Pharisee" once we look beyond his shaved scalp, his tattoos, her motorcycle helmet, the safety pins in her nose—or their wash-and-wear button-down polyester uniform that I disdain? Jesus spends a great deal of time on this character, naming him first one way and then her another. Such human beings are not far from most of us, I suspect, their typical behaviors very difficult to avoid. How so?

All "they" do is take an inventory, after all, whose purpose is to leave them feeling gratified. In so doing they risk undercounting the neighbor's goods and inflating the stock of their own. We when like them are inclined to choose categories where we excel compared to the others (in our view) and then to make the discrepancy quite favorable to ourselves. There is little point in assessing if we are not going to come out well! And since our first step inevitably is to choose the categories, which again are likely to favor our own estimation of our virtues, we are deciding for God what are the fundamental priorities. So the exercise is not only fruitless but badly misleading since we learn nothing of ourselves and end up obscuring what there is to see in the first place.

Additionally, the areas around which we organize our demonstration of near-perfection are not only the ones where we are liable to be myopic about the others and eutopic about ourselves; the presumed healthy and virtuous conditions under self-scrutiny are quite plausibly the very ones where we are vulnerable ourselves. It is the point Jesus makes so visibly with the two sons of the prodigal father: the older boy feels above the sins he lists on his brother's scorecard without hearing that in desiring to corner goods he is much like the one he despises. Perhaps, to discuss the Pharisee rather than ourselves, he has some fundamental dis-ease about his observances, resents tithing but does it anyway, is a secret glutton but makes himself do the optional fasts. In this case his enumeration of his virtues hides many times over an insight about himself in relation to both God and neighbor that might, if he could get at it, help him be more authentic, more like the rest of the human race. So we may feel at first, listening to the self-revelation of this man, that we are not like him at all, are not a Pharisee but an anti-establishment liberal from the opposite side. It is just then that we most need to look again.

The problem is not primarily his lists. It is rather his non-searching face, his announcement that certain things are just not likely in his situation. And out from the Temple he goes, asking nothing, getting nothing. But if we return to the lineup we may provide an alternate ending to the parable—or rather an ending to the gap it left. Once we discover from the lineup that the one who mugs us is not always the others but at least sometimes ourselves, that is our starting point. And then, desperate and shamed—which is how we may feel once we see ourselves guilty in the lineup—at the very moment when prayer (search) is farthest from our felt need, we may begin.

Our search for the face of God goes on, even surrounded as we are by those who threaten us, who let us down; if we look very carefully we may even identify them as our "other half," our self-sufficient, entitlement-seeking, account-keeping self that interrupts our prayer and undermines our confidence. Those who know our faces best may find that we toggle among these alternatives with surprising ease. Maybe we can at times scarcely tell the difference between the suspects! But in any case, whichever face it is that shows up to pray, we present it before the face of God. We do not arrive at one or other of those places in one big jump usually, but by many small steps. Genuine change, conversion, is not easy, not simply a matter of deciding and rooting out some flimsy weed from our garden. So we mention it again. "Take care of that, please! My heart reminds you. . . ." Reactivate us, bring us back to the Temple, to the rock of help, as our less exalted selves. We do not demand to be cured from such attitudes, though such a gift may be given. We simply bring it to our prayer, let our faces speak it forth. Perhaps we pray to live without our comparative ruler that so tempts us to measure others' pathetic gaps and our own proud and muscular bulges.

Five people come up to the Temple to pray. God's face wants to be seen, hidden though it may seem. God is eager that we seek the faces, the facets of God's goodness, that these become mirrored into our faces so that others may be drawn as well, drawn as we have been by the faces we have examined here. God's elusiveness and attractiveness are related to the rhythms of our search, and whom we resemble and what we see in the faces of others is related to our search for the face providing security.

NOTES: CHAPTER 4

[1]Luke has given the parable a label, which is of course very apt: "He also told this parable to some who trusted in themselves that they were righteous and regarded others with contempt." But before we construe the parable solely in terms of the setting Luke has supplied let us see what we can come up with ourselves. It will not likely fall too far from what Luke prescribes.

[2]There are a number of recent studies offering much-needed information on the Judaisms around the general time of Jesus. One useful work is that of Anthony J. Saldarini, *Pharisees, Scribes and Sadducees in Palestinian Society: A Sociological Approach* (Wilmington: Michael Glazier, 1988).

[3]Resetting this parable a little is particularly important since the term "Pharisee" is so intrinsically associated with Judaism. It has been all too automatic to assume that the parable is a condemnation of observant Judaism, a comfortable conclusion for any of us insofar as we do not understand the details of Pharisaic observance very well and may be blind to our own equivalent modes. In so concluding we do a double disservice: missing the point for ourselves and reinforcing a negative conclusion about the religious practice of Jesus' time or thereabouts.

[4]Hebrew perceptively has no singular of the noun. "Faces" is always plural since in fact each of us rotates a collection.

[5]Megan McKenna, *Parables. The Arrows of God* (Maryknoll, N.Y.: Orbis, 1994), whose valuable insights on the parables are practical and pointed, discusses this parable in her chapter 5. She suggests that to any poor woman these two men would look surprisingly similar. I simply clothe her suggestion with the specific dress of the widow of Luke 21:1-4.

[6]Since the Hebrew text does not use quotation marks it is difficult to peel off the layers of language in v. 8: the Hebrew text says, "seek (plural) my face," which a note suggests emending to "seek (singular) his face." The referents are ambiguous so we need to construe as best we can.

5

Entitlement and Responsiveness: Psalm 18 and Luke 18:1-8

S ome nature metaphors like the tree, or aspectual ones like stature and visage, are sufficiently sharp and decisive that once we have spotted them our track is relatively clear. Others are less obvious or definitive and require some preliminary negotiation before we can get down to the metaphorical processes themselves. Such is the case with the figure we will name "entitlement and responsiveness." This metaphor allows us fresh access to our expectations when we pray.

A practical preliminary procedure for working with psalms and parables is to map them in order to discern where they are heading. This initial organizing step is especially helpful with a psalm that is long and detailed—surely the case with Psalm 18—and with a parable very succinct and liable to be lost or overshadowed—which threatens in Luke 18:1-8. As we lay these texts out we attend of necessity to their details and watch for the play of the metaphor. Each of the two texts to be examined in this chapter shares an explicit *context*, a initial *problem*, a *cry for help*, a *response*, *basis for the response*, and a *result*. Once the structuring elements of these texts have been ordered and can be seen as parallel we will more easily engage the metaphor that will guide us to the depths that lie underneath the neat surfaces of these two biblical pieces.

An aerial reconnaissance of both psalm and parable will get us started this time. The context provided for us in the superscription of the psalm (Ps 18:1) is King David's flight from his various enemies (notably Saul), his rescue by God, and his praise of God for the assistance.[1]

David, or the psalmist, or any of us entering this psalm begins with an acknowledgment of what has occurred, with what can be anticipated to recur:

> I love you, God, my strength,
> my rock, my shelter, my stronghold.
> My God, I lean on you,
> my shield, my rock,
> my champion, my defense.
> When I call for help, I am safe from my enemies.
> Praise to the Lord! (Ps 18:1-4).

Luke begins the parable we are about to hear by telling us something similar: its context and meaning. The evangelist begins, "Then Jesus told them a parable about their need to pray always and not to lose heart" (18:1). That is, Luke tells us before Jesus speaks that the parable is about persistence in prayer and confidence in response. The initial information in both texts helps us locate the heart of what is to be unfolded for us—or better, shows us a place of entrance to the rich foliage of these two narratives. Such information, though direct, leaves us considerable room in which to maneuver, given our many situations of opposition and need for help. We need not be a besieged monarch or a disadvantaged widow to find these words helpful, but simply needy humans who may sometimes become fearful.

Each text next moves quickly to describe the *problem* or particular situation of need that brings forth the *call for help*. Psalm 18:5-7 vividly pictures the creep of evil toward the psalmist:

> Death had me in its grip,
> The current swept me away;
> Sheol was closing in,
> I felt the hand of death.
> From the depths I cried out,
> my plea reached the heavens.
> God heard me (Ps 18:5-7).

The danger is pictured clearly: death or some evil whose precise nature is not yet clarified sneaks up, grasps me, hangs on tight, sweeps off with me firmly in tow. The threat surrounds, undermines, confronts, comes near to completing its mission. Like an inexorable tide coming closer, higher, inch by inch, or like a menacing shadow looming suddenly, death and the underworld of Sheol threaten to reverse all that is vital and relational. The person who piles up these images feels vulnerable to some considerable extent. But when he cries out, though perhaps late in the process, the raised voice finds its mark; God's ear catches the thrown cry.

Jesus moves as quickly to set forth the problem situation he wishes to recount: "He said, 'In a certain city there was a judge who neither feared God nor had respect for people. In that city there was a widow who kept coming to him and saying, "Grant me justice against my opponent"'" (Luke 18:2-3).

We can detect a similarity with the psalm: some crisis whose particulars remain unvoiced but open to our imaginations, a problem that threatens the widow. Like the psalmist she cries out for help. As soon as we hear the voice of the widow pleading on her own behalf we register that at least part of her need is brought about by lack of helpers among her own kin: no husband and evidently no children who take up her cause. A single tag, "widow," helps us picture her as alone, needy, desperate, necessarily determined to get a response. And so out of her extreme circumstances and lack of alternatives she speaks up.

Both texts move quickly to detail the *response* to the outcry. The psalm explores it in what might seem almost a parody of our wildest hopes.

> Then the earth shook;
> the mountains quaked,
> they rocked from side to side,
> trembled at God's anger.
> With fiery breath and blazing nostrils
> God split open the heavens,
> coming down on dense clouds,
> riding on the cherubim throne,
> soaring aloft with the winds.
> Cloaked in darkness,
> concealed in the rainstorm,
> with flaming clouds,
> with hail and coals of fire,
> the Lord almighty
> thundered from the heavens,
> aimed lightning bolts like arrows
> to rout the enemy.
> At your rebuke, Lord,
> when you bellowed in fury,

the bed of the ocean,
the foundations of the earth,
were laid bare.
From on high God took hold of me,
lifted me clear of the deadly waters (Ps 18:8-17).

One call to God, no matter how late, secures not only instant but over-whelming response: massive, manifold, millennial. The earth itself re-verberates its tectonic plates, its mountains roil their molten depths. The heavens, splitting like a curtain to let God appear visibly on the stage, contribute their own special effects: lightning illuminates heavy cloud cover, rain and hail pellets beat down. Wind and wave wrestle so fiercely in the ocean beds that the very foundations of the earth are un-covered. Then God arrives, dismounts from a fiery chariot, and reaches to pluck the psalmist—ourselves—from the chasm in which we are about to be swallowed: just in time, but with the implication that the end has never been in doubt. God's response is instant, thorough, un-mistakable. God, aided by the powerful elemental facets of nature, in-tervenes on the side of the petitioner. The deity, habitually hidden in nature, reveals self at the key moment.

Here the parable diverges radically in content though not in form. The response to the widow's prayer is narrated as no response. Jesus notes, "'For a while he refused . . .'" (Luke 18:4a). If we flesh out this spare and cryptic scene we can imagine the persistent widow hanging around the judge's house, asserting her petition whether verbally or silently, her need thus made explicit not only to herself, to the judge, and possibly to her invisible opponent, but to us as well. In a shame so-ciety like that presumed in the gospels where the widow's persistent presence—her lawn chair and sleeping bag—are a public reproach to the judge the implication of criticism would be clear to all who are part of their community.[2] The narrator—Jesus in this case—has already told us that the judge cares little for the opinion of God or the esteem of humans, a situation that makes the widow's plight all the more des-perate. What can possibly motivate justice if not divine or human re-spect? A judge so untouchable that he need not take into account what God or his own community thinks of him is not likely to be approach-able by a widow, who weighs little on the scale compared to the parties on whom the judge so disdainfully turns his back.

The psalmist goes on to reflect on the *reasons for the response* just experienced:

My raging foes were strong,
stronger than I,
but God rescued me.
They rushed at me
on the day of disaster,
but the Lord upheld me.
God snatched me free,
led me to where I could breathe.
The Lord loved me.
I was just,
my hands were clean,
so the Lord rewarded me.
I have kept the commandments,
the laws set before me,
followed the path laid down,
never turned aside from my God.
I am without blame,
I have kept myself from evil.
The Lord gives me a just reward,
because my hands are clean.
To those who are faithful
you are faithful,
with those who are honest
you are candid.
To the just you show goodness,
with the perverse you are cunning.
You rescue the humble,
the mighty are brought low.
My God, you are my light,
a lamp for my darkness.
With strength from you, Lord,
I charge the enemy,
I climb their ramparts.
God, your way is perfect,
your word is fire-tried.
You shield all who seek refuge.
Who is God but the Lord?
Who is the rock but our God? (Ps 18:18-32).

The basis for the divine response seems, at first consideration, to be fairly clear. The victorious assistance described is given because or insofar as the psalmist is deserving of help and the opponents of disaster. Asking on the basis of relationship, the psalmist expects the response detailed. Why would God not help? How could God have any conflict about this particular situation of need? The psalmist's self-assessment is clear, sentiments we can perhaps echo with some confidence: justice-oriented, clean-handed, law-respectful, blameless, faithful, honest, humble. God is attentive to such persons; on that we wish to rely. God's qualities correspond to, reinforce, and sustain those of the petitioner.

The parable similarly moves on to the factors involved in the eventual response. Though the judge has not paid much attention to the widow so far, which is to say he has refused to assist her, he has been affected. Jesus shows the judge finally bestirring himself though still maintaining a portrait quite remote from that of the psalm: "'. . . but later he said to himself, "Though I have no fear of God and no respect for anyone, yet because this widow keeps bothering me, I will grant her justice, so that she may not wear me out by continually coming"'" (Luke 18:4b-5). Reiterating in his own soliloquy what Jesus has already told us, talking only to himself and certainly not to the woman, the judge acts solely in light of his own convenience. The specifics of his eventual action are not even recited by Jesus except in summary. What the judge says about his own response—the widow does not comment on it!—is that it proceeds precisely from the non-relationship the man claims with everyone else in the community and from the non-entanglement that he wishes to enter more absolutely with the widow.

The *outcomes* of the two narratives wind up each recital. The psalmist moves on in imagery that may resound in our ears as excessive to describe his own enlistment on the side of God in the battle:

> Armed with your strength,
> my way is sure.
> You make me swift as a deer,
> bounding over the hills.
> You train me for combat,
> teach me to draw a mighty bow.
> You gave me your shield for victory,
> supported me with your right hand,
> made me strong with your might.
> I march out boldly,
> my stride is firm.
> I overtake my enemies,
> not turning back
> until they are no more.
> I strike them down,

they lie dead at my feet.
You arm me for battle,
my enemies collapse.
I step on their necks
to destroy them.
They cry for help
but there is none,
they cry to the Lord,
but the Lord does not answer.
I grind them fine
as wind-blown dust,
toss them out
like rubbish in the streets.
You saved me from invaders,
made me ruler over the nations.
Foreign people serve me.
They hear me and obey,
they cringe before me.
Exhausted and trembling,
they crawl out from hiding.
The Lord lives!
blessed be my rock,
the God who saves me,
the God who avenges,
who makes the nations submit.
You humble my foes,
from the violent you rescue me.
Among the nations I praise you,
sing your power and name.
You give great victory
to your anointed king,
you are faithful for all time
to the house of David (Ps 18:33-51).

Turning, once assisted, from beleaguered to triumphant, the psalmist describes himself and perhaps us as now recruited into the heavenly ranks. Trained in swift footwork and for treading to string the bow, enclosed by a protective shield, we move to the offensive. The corpses of those who were dragging us by the ankles down to Sheol pile up beneath us now where we stamp them fine and sweep them with our feet out into the street like trash for the pickup. Those few who survive we subdue, praising God as the source of our accomplishments. Exuberant detail accumulates as we conclude our prayer.

Luke notes that Jesus, more economical with words, wraps up the parable on a not dissimilar note as follows: "'Listen to what the unjust judge says. And will not God grant justice to his chosen ones who cry to him day and night? Will he delay long in helping them? I tell you, [God] will quickly grant justice to them . . .'" (Luke 18:6-8a). Count on God's speedy responsiveness and move into its circle quickly, Jesus seems to advise, referring us back to the words of the judge. And we may now wish to ask: what words of the judge? What is it we are instructed to hear from him; why are we needing to listen to what he says? Having sorted these texts, put them in dialogue with each other and with us, we can see several things more clearly.

Perhaps our own experience has welled up undeniably by now, ready for us to examine before we resume our exploration of these two passages. The word "entitlement" is key and familiar in these days. The most obvious referent is civic and social: our payment of taxes is made with the expectation that we get services in return; our willingness to contribute to retirement systems is predicated on our understanding that we will in time recoup money. The government has made a contract it must endeavor to keep. A commitment—mutual—is presumed and able to be called on at the right moment. The notion of entitlement is pervasive in other realms as well, though sometimes less explicitly. Parents, aging, expect some care and consideration from capable children. Employees with seniority and achievement do not anticipate termination from the companies long and well served. Countries receiving military assistance may seem churlish when they train the weapons upon the providers. We even occasionally encounter street people who feel entitled to what they can get from more affluent passersby, the feeling obvious to eye or ear when the funds are not forthcoming and even sometimes when they are.

The level of our expectation may be gauged by the degree of fear we exhibit when our promised or anticipated goods are threatened, when the responsiveness does not quite match what we feel owed. What stands in the way of our getting what we are owed? Alas, it is "the others" as usual, with their needs, their desires, their own sense of deservingness—all of which often seem inflated to us. Their getting theirs may interfere with our getting ours, and of course the mere phrasing reveals something of the problem. People like ourselves, normally kind and rational, can become unexpectedly impervious to alternatives when these fears mount up, and not always without cause. Let us go now to a deeper reflection on the psalm and parable and see what the metaphor of entitlement and responsiveness, fleshed out in Scripture in military and juridical situations, offers us by way of redescription of our relationship with God. We can note five points.

First we can see that we have been given by both texts not individual portraits of a responding deity, whether cosmic warrior or dishonest judge, but rather two group pictures, perhaps even a pair of short videos, showing responsive relationships. We can see them as two circles each including ourselves, God, and our opponents, with no allies or other extras to confuse us. The metaphor involves not simply God as warrior or judge and us as desperate petitioner; rather we are given two short clips on entitlement and responsiveness and asked to find ourselves and God and our opponents in one or both groupings, which is our second point to explore.

It may initially seem unlikely, given our choices. In a common setting of crisis we are offered in the mirror a king and a widow, two opposite ends of the sociopolitical and economic spectrum. The Davidic kings, adopted as God's sons, are bound to God by pacts, share with God the responsibility for doing justice in the realm; the widow and judge are likewise bound together by the fact that the leadership whose justice the official represents is made responsible for her special plight. But we might feel little in common with either of these figures, positioning ourselves somewhat closer to the middle of the spectrum at whose ends these two stand. We are not so privileged as the king nor so marginal as the widow. Our choices for identifying ourselves seem too extreme.

Similarly we can watch the same extremes of reaction to our royal or reduced crisis: the heavenly warrior with a wild exuberance and the corrupt judge with grudging disdain and minimal involvement. Perhaps again our experiences of adjudicating authority fall between this pair. That is precisely the point. Our juxtapositioning of these two texts generates for us merisms, end points, extremes within which to situate ourselves. As the expressions "a to z" or "soup to nuts" imply not only the end elements but everything intervening, so the extremities of these sketches push us back toward the middle of the spectrum. The military and judicial metaphor of entitlement and responsiveness explores several questions: who asks and why, who responds and on what basis, with what results?

Third, it becomes clear that in each text there is a third character forming the relationship of entitlement and responsiveness. Once we can see that there is a circle of participants we have to notice the opponents of the psalmist and the almost invisible person (or set) who has wronged the widow. That they are indicated in outline and not well detailed gives us scope in determining them more fully. All they do is oppose. The details of opposition are not important and can be filled in as desired; they are not the main point. Between petitioner and petitioned in each case stands one neither asking help nor asked for it but representing a potential claim on warrior and judge. The others, by their mere presence, threaten the equilibrium of what we anticipate. Their function in these two texts is to trigger the demand or the need for response, thus laying bare the dynamic of expectation. The merisms for the other character sets—the king and the widow, the warrior and the judge—direct our attention to the common element defining the opponent: refusal to relate in any positive or constructive way. They simply oppose.

Fourth, we can examine now more closely what the royal psalmist and the litigating widow request from their benefactors and what in fact they get. The psalmist, facing death or its near equivalent, asks for stability. Calling God names like rock, shelter, stronghold, asking for a steady surface against which to lean or within which to stand, hoping to be lifted up and repositioned on something firm: the psalmist and we alongside him picture God as reliable and unyielding, as though that is what we most desire and need. And what we get in this particular text is therefore quite startling: motion. God the rock grinds tectonic plates and shakes up everything resting upon them; God makes mountains teeter, spilling off their sides any thinking themselves settled. The divine warrior re-scrambles the elements of the universe while aiding the king. The response, unexpected in terms of stability, is constant motion: coming down, riding, soaring, aiming, laying bare, scooping, lifting.

The parable is similar. The widow wants justice. As a widow, at least under Old Testament law, she can anticipate special concern from God and from the community. Along with orphans and sojourners[3] she receives, if not structural change that might come closer to ending her permanent state of poverty and dependency, at least legal privileges that (theoretically) alleviate it on a regular basis. But expecting and desiring justice, she gets from the judge instead a crooked decision, a corrupt ruling little relevant to her case. That she may be in the right becomes almost unimportant in the text, moot for the judge as he makes his decision. Like the psalmist she receives the opposite of the justice she demands. Neither petitioner appears displeased. As noted above, the psalmist gloats rather unpleasantly over the outcome of his particular appeal to the rock, and the widow, vanishing from the gospel story line, is hardly likely to refuse the long-awaited verdict on the basis of flawed procedure, which of course she does not know since the judge makes his ruling in soliloquy. Will each be back to petition again?

A fifth and very important point, bringing us finally to the heart of the metaphor, is the basis for the request of each petitioner and for the response of the petitioned. Entitlement and responsiveness form an encircling bond that works dialectically and reciprocally and cannot really be split into "petitioned" and "petitioner." How do we ask or claim response from our helper? Why do we yield to those who lay claim on our resources? Again what we see is two extremes. The psalmist seems to ask on the basis of familiarity. The implication seems to be that he and God have a past together. The psalmist rings, confident of response, having coded God's phone number to a quick-dial, so well-used is it, so often rung. The psalmist feels very free to ask for help. God responds—has responded, will respond—not only on the basis of extreme need but because of what has gone before. Though we may read the claims of integrity (vv. 20-26) as pride or presumption they are equally revealing as past shared adventures. Our reminiscences to God: "keeping the commandments . . . following the path . . . never turning aside . . ." are themselves metaphors for our struggle to live the details of life within the framework God has set, and as such reflect our efforts at integrity. It is not so much presumptuous entitlement that is alleged here as it is confidence that, based on past performance, God is likely to respond. How does anyone claim what the psalmist claims except in the company of strong support?

The widow's feelings are less clear to us since she speaks but a sentence. Her behavior of persistent petition, however, underlines her sense of expectation. Justice is lacking; the judge is in the position to bestow it on her, so she—not running the risk of getting his voice mail, or more likely not having access to his number—goes to present her request in person. Worn out by the injustice she is suffering, she plans to wear him out as well, or so he fears. He owes her justice and she deserves it. Has the widow selected the judge from choice or from need? And for all that the judge and the narrator deny it we can see that the widow has in fact gotten through to the judge, not so much on the basis of his integrity or her entitlement but on the basis of past behavior.

These are gross images for our relationship with God but their very exaggeration is what gets our attention. In fact to recognize the caricature helps free us from taking the images as other than metaphoric. No less than the tree, the entitlement-responsiveness dynamic needs to be laid next to our relationship with God and neighbor, then sorted according to what describes us compellingly and what does not. The speakers of these texts, we must recognize, are feeling some urgency. David is not short of moments of desperation as he flees his various foes and Jesus may easily be imagined as having a sense of running out of time as he approaches Jerusalem, whatever specific fate he may anticipate meeting there. These two experienced storytellers are offering not simple crayon portraits of God but dynamic scenarios of how the connections work among ourselves, God, and our opponents. It is the circuitry we need to eye here. How can these outsized and shriveled relationship metaphors give us insight? What fits, and more important, what is jarring, and why? When we screen our relationships with God through the filters of king calling to cosmic warrior for reinforcements and of wronged woman making innumerable appeals to wronging judge, what lingers to inform us and what falls ineffectually to the side?

Our experience will again be key. Religion for many people is an economy of entitlement. Deals are made, investments risked, gains anticipated. Some people may quit the market when they lose too heavily or too often but even their storming out indicates their sense of the system that let them down. Others stay in, fingering their accumulations, sounding more like the psalmist in his final verses than like the widow who goes off in a more inscrutable silence. Is deservingness really the key to these texts? Are our moral lives, our good deeds and our regular good behaviors like a sort of foreign aid we dole out to God, counting on a loyal response when trouble strikes our realm? Are our manageable situations the result of grudging justice meted out by God who might have done the same for others were they as persistent and deserving as ourselves? We may prefer not to recognize our own contract when it is stated so baldly. But the crassness of the formulation offers us clear lines within which to ask some key questions. How closely do these terms fit what we expect or demand? Entitlement and responsiveness offer us an inconvenient mirror.

Or is there another possibility, still fitting within the reciprocal bond of past experience and relationship? On whom do we prefer to call, if we have a choice when we need something urgently, a cup of flour while baking a dessert that needs to rise or a pint of blood when we are scheduled for surgery? When desperate do we call on those who "owe" us or on those who have been helpful in the past, are our proven friends, whether our account is in the black or the red at the moment?

When most in trouble will we make our situation known to those who keep score—and with whom we feel the need to keep track—or to those with whom we are beyond such a point? How many friends have our number taped to the wall above their phones so they can call us quickly when trouble descends, with no real calculation of how the take-give score stands at the moment the call needs to be placed? And how do we respond to such requests when they arrive, and arrive again?

Our own experience on both ends of the entitlement-responsiveness spectrum and occurring repeatedly within its giving-receiving spirals will help us catch the most vital aspect of these texts: the quality of the shared past. Is our relationship with God such that we can call? want to call? will call confidently? honestly? If not, why not? Does our need seem too hopeless even for God? Do we hate to admit we are in trouble? Is it simply too painful, too embarrassing, to begin the request? Do we pretend it is too much of a bother for God's busy self? Do we perhaps, or many people we know, have whole files in our mental storage cabinets of God's failures to respond? We have called and gotten no help. Or we may feel that God, as agent or perpetrator of the very vicissitudes we wish alleviated, is hardly the help we most wish to see should God chance to show up. The psalmist's exuberance at God's response gives us occasion to reflect on our own expectations. The widow, who turns out to know the judge better than he knows himself, offers a profile at the other end of the spectrum. The king and the widow, each for opposite reasons, have no doubt that the petitioned one will respond, and their confidence, built up from past experience, moves them to act as they do. Asking is constitutive of receiving, and giving help engenders the request for it. The point is the quality of the relationship, not simply its isolated factors.

Though each reader will need to ask these questions and offer responses repeatedly because the metaphor is elusive, let me offer one sorting of its possible insight for us. Action from God is desirable especially when it comes on the basis of what we have already cultivated in our past doings. The intimacy of feeling free to mention any need, no matter how vulnerable it shows us to be, our confidence of gaining some return from the one we address, fits the metaphor of entitlement-responsiveness well. God is there to be asked; it is part of God's "job description" to respond. Our creatureliness and our sense of God's creative capacities shape the relationship in which we ask for what we require. Receiving something will encourage us to ask again. We will be pleased and God will be gratified as well. That much is, I think, fairly clear and comfortable.

But, upon my examination at least, almost everything else in the entitlement-responsiveness metaphor is jarring and semantically impertinent in this pair of texts. The extremes of the imagery are too shocking once laid bare. Those petitioned respond, though providing the opposite of what we ask. Though a reaction is forthcoming and we may ultimately get what we want we have lost control of the process. Responsiveness sounds desirable if we are at the controls. If not, it is frightening. But when we are at the controls is God responding? In our experience I venture to say there are some who speak with absolute assurance of God's signals or answers to them, calls or confirmations of one sort or another; they represent one extreme. And there are as many who claim never to have gotten so much as a syllable from God, whom they experience to be as discreet as a spectator at an auction, stifling shrugs and twitches and eyebrow lifts lest they result in the purchase of a Van Gogh. Does God respond or not?

Prompting us to consider carefully our own expectations may be the most valuable service the metaphor can perform. When we or people we know ask God for good weather, good luck, good health, tangible assists and justice, what precisely do we and they expect? What image of God lies behind such requests once we really stop to think of it? We end up, at least in these two texts, as agents of our own assistance, the psalmist shortly enlisted to do his own gory battle with opponents, the widow seeming to earn her justice simply by hanging around. We do not, I suspect, feel comfortable with either such a total and quick response or with the arbitrary and delayed one. The blend— or better, the merism—becomes disquieting, leading down to the next level of the question at hand. How does God respond? What do we understand God's responsiveness to comprise?

The survival and popularity of the image of God as supplying what we demand from lists that we make and present is surprising. That it continues to be powerful in the lives of so many people who presumably have frequent disappointments or at least uncertainties testifies to the strength with which we hold to it. Whether we anticipate that God will give us what we feel entitled to or whether we write off God for failing to do so matters little, really; the metaphor's dynamic is the same: entitlement and responsiveness. It is often noted as a great scandal that God did not intervene to stop the Holocaust or, we could add, the many other human catastrophes of our times and the countless preceding ones of which we know or care little. But I wonder if such intervention is really the best response of the cosmic warrior even as Psalm 18 asserts it through the victorious mouth of the psalmist. The dissonance of God heaping up corpses of our enemies and enabling us to do so is a major one, and the picture of God as a selfish old judge resenting but offering adjudication on the basis of a desire for undisturbed isolation should caution us.

Though I have not ceased to discuss in prayer the things that compose my day and the short run of my life—perhaps the weather, the outcome of a vote, my capacity or incapacity to perform well, the needs of those I love—it becomes clearer to me that I do not expect a tangible response. The arrival of the cosmic warrior leaping off a cloud like a Hell's Angel would shock me considerably, as would access to the ruminations of the curmudgeonly and crooked judge. Does such a conclusion on my part suggest that I have demoted and diminished God's power or that my imagination and generosity have shrunk imperceptibly until I am satisfied with the status quo, more or less? Matthew Kelty's admonition re-presents itself: if the psalms make us uncomfortable perhaps it is because we do not live where they live, do not want what they so desperately and flamboyantly picture us as wanting. The responsiveness-entitlement metaphor challenges us to persistent reexamination of our relationships.

Is it sufficient, satisfactory, necessary simply to turn our lives over to God's care without much counting or counting on the particulars of the outcome? Is the relationship more valuable than any accrued goods? Is the question sufficient or must we track it a little farther? Are we entitled simply to ask and is God eager to respond with strength and presence of some kind that we may or may not recognize as what we desired? Perhaps David the psalmist and Jesus the parabler can help us a bit more here, since it is their words initiating our central question of what we expect from and with God.

David, if we can allow him to be the speaker of Psalm 18 as the superscription suggests, seems contented with what he has gotten. But if we look elsewhere in his biblical life there is plenty more to pray about. Jesus, similarly, seems often in the gospels to ask God for assistance in cures and exorcisms and to be heard; indeed he encourages us to imitate him on similar occasions. But his biblical life as well is strewn with situations he must have prayed about repeatedly, constantly. It is difficult to imagine that he did not pray for the Jewish leaders who in the gospels dog him so relentlessly and whom he seems to have been incapable of reaching. He divulges that he does indeed pray for his closest friends, who seem to benefit minimally from it—at least rated on scales of visible achievement. Jesus, asking for and granting many things, is not given all.

Prayer may not be primarily for what we get from it except insofar as we get a strengthened relationship. The circles of these texts—God, ourselves, our opponents—continually move us along. Whom do we ask and why? who asks us and why? How do we ask, for what do we ask, with whose needs in mind do we continue to petition? If we feel God is non-responsive do we cease to dial the number? If we run out of needs of our own can we ask for others, perhaps even for our opponents? Do we reposition our needs among theirs, their demands in the midst of our own contentments? Such is the whirl of this metaphor of entitlement and responsiveness.

One last valuable point may be offered here, again from the excellent readings offered by Megan McKenna.[4] Her suggestion, fitting in with other moves we have made when reading these texts as metaphors rather than as allegories, is to consider shifting character roles. Though Jesus is not averse to using shocking images to introduce us to new depths of insight about God and ourselves and so could liken God to an unjust judge, might God also be suggested by the figure of the widow? As McKenna draws the implication the divine widow is the one who tugs day and night at the gown of our indifference, asking relentlessly that we do justice whether we feel like it or not, threatening to wear us out until we respond. And we can be certain since we have said even a grudging "yes" once that she will be back again with other urgent demands. Our relationship will build us gradually as God feels encouraged to press us for more and we become more eager to respond.

NOTES: CHAPTER 5

[1]Virtually the same text is inserted in the narrative story of David and various opponents told in 1–2 Samuel; the adventures of David culminate in this prayer uttered near the end of his life (2 Samuel 22). The superscriptions on some of the psalms, like the choices made by Luke for Jesus' teachings, are valuable and privileged but need not restrict our considering the words in other contexts.

[2]The implications of recognizing the honor-shame society are sketched in Bruce J. Malina and Richard L. Rohrbaugh, *A Social-Scientific Commentary on the Synoptic Gospels* (Minneapolis: Augsburg Fortress, 1992) 387 and passim. They remind us that honor and shame are not primarily feelings of individuals but almost tangible social commodities, limited in supply and publicly ascribable. When the widow calls such attention to the judge's lack of response she

in fact affects his status with the community, a fact his behavior if not his words makes clear.

[3]The laws that provide the general background for such an understanding can be found in Exod 22:21-27; Deut 23:15-16; Leviticus 25. The precise functioning of such laws as well as many questions underlying them are debated by scholars but the truism is that widows could expect special help.

[4]*Parables. The Arrows of God*, 105–06.

6

The Ecosystem: Psalm 7 and Luke 16:1-9

The image of God as harsh authority figure pronouncing arbitrary decisions and meting out heavy punishments and light rewards is pervasive in the minds and hearts of many people. It often gains strength from the parable just explored, where Jesus (or Luke) may imply or readers infer that God shares similarities with an unfair and arbitrary oppressor. Additionally and perniciously it is a sense of God that can lie functioning but unrecognized until a moment of crisis. Then a stern and powerful divine figure emerges from hiding and acts, rarely to the consolation of the human being in trouble at the time.

Conversely, even simultaneously, we may have another picture of a divine paramedic, a sort of 911 to be dialed when we are really desperate, someone at the other end of the phone whom we do not really know but who we expect will have to help us out when we phone in; after all, we pay taxes to keep such a system at the ready. Why should it not help us? This sense of God also emerges blinking into the light of day, as it were, rustled up out of hibernation almost instinctively by us or by people we know who feel out of nearer or likelier options. And though the on-call paramedic image may not seem too closely related to the stern judge, I think in fact they are both figures who help us dodge responsibility and relationship, who tempt us to live unproductively and only for the short term in our human and moral environment. To dread the one and presume truculently upon the latter is not the best we can do.

Many people bring forward from childhood a similar and dual image of parents: their supervision was dreaded on certain occasions but their care desired strongly on others; our need was to hide from their powerful scrutiny in some situations but to be watched approvingly in others. We are often not certain until a particular moment arrives which of the facets we are anticipating, which we are fearing, and why. These doubled images of God can be helpful and are surely classic in our texts. But when taken too literally or to the exclusion of many other images, when lifted out of a broader environment they are paralyzing, intimidating, and harmful. God as judge is prominent in Scripture and beloved in art, but to live in fear of the judge because we are uncomfortable with the terms of divine justice is not healthy. To cry from our creatureliness is most appropriate and is encouraged repeatedly in biblical texts, but to ignore health persistently and then expect a miracle from the paramedics is unrealistic and childish. So also, to switch images, is our fearing and hoping to avoid an inspection visit from the fire department while ignoring the growth of dry brush and debris around our wooden homes, materials that will feed flames on the day a hot and heedless wind brings fire near us. The fire brigade may be helpless to prevent consequences we might have sooner attended to ourselves—with their encouragement, of course. Just as in the last chapter we entered the metaphor of entitlement and responsiveness to perceive something freeing about our expectations of God, so we can do a similar thing here in terms of our moral lives.

What we shall attempt now is to bring some facets of a larger environment forward so that we can consider our human capacities for responsible actions and ethical choices more clearly in relationship to and in greater alignment with the matrices in which we live. The metaphor of the ecosystem can help us reposition the figure of the authoritative element or governance behind it—whether arbiter to be feared or helper to be desired—and ourselves as judged for infraction or needy of assistance. There is no image under consideration among these psalms and parables where there is greater need to distinguish carefully the features of the metaphor that work productively from those that do not and to examine the apparent dissonance with great care. A result of our doing so will be to envision ourselves as functioning in an interactive network rather than simply as targets of others' malign or benign choices, God's included. The metaphor of the ecosphere, describing freshly and well the situation in which we find ourselves repeatedly, will show us something valuable about moral terrain and make visible some things we may be missing.

The ecosystem is familiar to us in a way it would not have been to our grandparents or perhaps even to our parents a generation ago. And though certain cultures are infinitely more aware of the delicate balance that composes the ecosphere than most citizens of the industrialized world have been, it has taken the carnage and detritus of highly technological processes to make the complex symbol of the environmental web truly visible to us. We have become aware of the interconnectedness of the habitat of nature in many ways, from tiny to vast, private to public. It is in the sickness of the environment, unfortunately, that we most clearly see the possibilities for health and the urgency of reformed choices. Some examples will help flesh out the range of the metaphor.

Certain reverberations are very clear: a nuclear catastrophe like the meltdown at Chernobyl affects the air above and around that site, the clouds bringing rain to its neighbors, the soil onto which their rain eventually falls, food produced there and shipped and eaten anywhere it is sold. Wendell Berry, who writes steadily on links between the environment and moral choices, shows the connections that are more positive. Making a sustainable city that purchases more of its food from its own agricultural countryside consequently enables local farming to become more diverse. Farms, smaller but more complex in structure, require labor that can be drawn from the city. Organic wastes from the city can in time go out to fertilize the farms.

> [T]hus city people would have to assume an agricultural responsibility and would be motivated to do so both by the wish to have a dependable supply of excellent food and by the fear of contaminating the supply. The increase of economic intimacy between a city and its sources would change minds . . . would improve minds. The locality, by becoming partly sustainable, would produce the thought it would need to become more sustainable.[1]

Our actions are always part of a larger system that contributes to their texture and that they affect as well, for ultimate gain or for loss. The ecosystem provides us also with many layers of situations and events temporally and causally related, but where cause and effect are not necessarily visible nor immediately traceable. We share a common habitat, participating in it at many levels. We do things that affect it beneficially and adversely, some of which we know, many of which we do not recognize. And we live in a system where others act too, affecting us as well as themselves positively and negatively, visibly and invisibly, immediately and much later. The ecosystem has its own processes and ways that are adaptable to our choices in some instances but not in all. Actions have myriad consequences outside those intended or preferred, often far beyond our control.

We may find ourselves to be in some sort of a crisis and the nature of our response can be instructive. How we envision the remediation tells us a great deal about our sense of ourselves as participants. When a major oil spill occurs, what are possible responses among those involved? Is the choice to avoid authorities who will critique and condemn our role in the catastrophe? or do we want to call for help? Is our concern mostly for ourselves, perhaps for our liability? or is there some thought for the needs of the others as well? Do we envision ourselves as part of the cleanup process or does it seem so overwhelming to us, or perhaps so remote from our shores, that we feel quite disconnected? How will we act so as to prevent another devastating event?

The metaphor of the ecosystem can provide a way to look at ourselves and our problems, our various "oil spills"—that is, situations in which we have some responsibility. Many of the psalms and parables can be examined in terms of this fundamental metaphor of the ecosystem. Psalm 7 and Jesus' parable of the unjust manager in Luke 16 are simply two of them. What this pair of texts offers us is, at the surface, a situation where someone is in trouble, embedded in pollution, is or feels unjustly thwarted by a malfunctioning environment, appeals for something that is withheld or hopes to avoid the consequences that seem imminent. In each narrative there is a "targeted" individual, an authority figure to whom appeal may be made, potential helpers or foes, and a roughly sketched scenario. The key pair to watch in each short narrative is the one in trouble and the one in some position of authority, able to help, ready to intervene. But we may also notice the systemic nature of the crisis. In the last chapter we examined the metaphor shaped by a petitioning king and widow and by a responding warrior and judge to seek redescription of ourselves as appealing to and assisted by God. Here we are looking at a related situation: the moral universe we share with God and other creatures, our choices, and God's assessments of them.

Let us plunge into the several scenarios of "sickness" or trouble that thread throughout Psalm 7:

> 2 You are my haven, Lord my God,
>   save me from my attackers.
>   Rescue me, their helpless prey;

  3 these lions will tear me to pieces.
  4 Lord, if I have done wrong,
      if there is guilt on my hands,
  5 if I have mistreated friend or foe
      for no good reason,
  6 then let the enemy hound me,
      overtake and kill me,
      trample my life to the ground. . . .
13 Instead they sharpen their swords,
      string their bows,
      and light flaming arrows,
14 taking up lethal weapons (Ps 7:2-6, 13-14).

The psalmist pictures herself and her opponents in several ways, characterizing their mutually constructed trouble in a pair of succeeding images. She is like a small animal attacked by larger ones, helpless against the ravening power of their jaws. They, for certain purposes of their own, are eager to rip her life to shreds, consume her completely. We can discern in this forest image the process of tracking, overtaking, trampling, killing, and the mounting terror experienced by the victim as the predator draws ever nearer. Part of what is made prominent here is the fear or possibility of abandonment of the hunted one, the potential absence of any help that would defer or deter the destruction. She cries out for help, her appeal mingled with the fear of non-response. In fact, as we will explore below, she even invites it as a possibility. What she has detailed, therefore, is a web of relationships connecting herself, God, and her enemies in which the actions of one have profound and varying effects upon the others.

Coming to reinforce that image is the enemy pictured in more specifically human terms. The technologically advanced and advantaged foes hone finer the metal weapons they possess, tread in order to string tall bows into readiness for the kill, ignite wads of flammable substance that will lead the arrows to a fiery destination; in short, the opponents array and ready the whole range of their arsenal against the one apparently helpless to defend herself. The enemy here is human rather than animal but shares with the previous image the sense of hounding the prey into submission, into non-being. Missing in this second image is the intimacy of the kill—the breath of the hound on the neck of the hare, the visibility and sound of the gleaming teeth and snapping jaws. But brought forward this time is the horror of destruction coming suddenly and from afar, perhaps unexpectedly, with no immediate warning. So we have a pair of related images in which the psalmist characterizes what is wrong in her environment. Both images suggest unfairness, mismatch, unevenness of the fight and the unlikelihood of survival of the weaker party.

The next image for evil rings a change on the predator image, again in a pair of figures:

> 15 See how they conceive evil,
>   grow pregnant with trouble,
>   and give birth to lies.
> 16 Sinners land in the pit
>   dug with their own hands.
> 17 Their evil crashes on their heads;
>   they are victims of their own violence.

Here it is the evildoers who reduplicate and reproduce their own nastiness: conceiving it in partnership, incubating and increasing it, nurturing it continuously, with care over time until it emerges, able to survive separated from its progenitors. Evil begets its own offspring that emerges fraudulent, untrue to its origins, turning on its parents. Similar is the notion that the wicked construct their own ruin. Their hands busily dig a pit with whatever hopes and plans in mind for others, but it is themselves that the pit collects, their malevolence crashing in on top of their own heads once they have fallen, their own violence catching them around the ankle and occasioning the slip and the fall. The psalmist has not here detailed the impact of the evil on others though we can hardly imagine that the young evil turns only on those who have hatched it, that the hidden pit catches only those who have dug and forgotten it.

The common factor to the verses may be the inevitability of the negative effect, the inexorability of destruction on all who come within its range. No more can the weaker animal escape the hunting predator or the besieged the eventual success of powerfully destructive weapons than does the perpetrator of wickedness avoid its engulfing effects. The two pairs of images for polluting evil offer us two ways of seeing the psalmist—or ourselves—as we explore the terrain here. In one case the distinction between good and evil is clear: the evil prey on the innocent. In the other set of images the wicked are additionally infected by the results of their own evil deeds. Intermingled with the description of the environmental catastrophe in the psalm is the psalmist's situating herself amidst it. Enemies hound her, shoot flaming arrows at her; has she hounded others, shot wads of fiery material into the wind, perhaps not recalling the dry brush that has crept up around her own house as she plans the destruction of their homes? She appeals to God for help, but she excuses God from the responsibility to answer if in fact she has acted unjustly toward others. At the moment of being pursued she ponders her pursuit of others. Aligning herself as clearly undeserving of what threatens her, she nevertheless explores the alternative as at least a possibility.

Finding herself innocent, she feels free to call to God. If she herself has been unjust in some way then she offers to remain at the non-mercy of those who wish her ill. If not, she expects and anticipates a rescue. Are a guilty pursuer and the innocent pursued as distinct as the first pair of images suggests, or is the pit a more realistic image? The fate of the guilty recoils on their own heads but not on theirs alone. Those who fall into the pit may recall that they shoveled the dirt out, leaving the hole, and that it was their hands that arranged a misleading surface. But they may have no awareness of it at all. Or they may be wholly innocent of the particular pit into which they tumble. At one level it matters not at all; at another level, greatly. We and they, the just and the unjust, all mingle in the pit into which we find ourselves fallen. Whatever our intent, whatever our portion of responsibility, we inherit the disaster. Evil, as it gets loose, penetrates the environment in which live the innocent, the guilty, and all those in between them. The psalm pictures it well in a series of quick scenarios.

We sell harmful petrochemicals to other nations for their crops, fertilizers that do not meet the safety standards for our own food-producing fields. Then unwittingly—strange though it may seem—we import the goods from those countries, food their own people may need more than we do, and end up ingesting the very molecules we hesitated to employ locally. Such toxicity affects the just and unjust alike. We may wonder how evildoers can have forgotten the placement of the pit on which they labored so hard, so as to tumble unawares into it. How can we be so little aware that we end up consuming indirectly and at some additional cost the substances that we feared to use? It is an amnesia that is illogical and irrational but common. To choose a simpler or more common example: we speak disparagingly and carelessly about those with whom we live and work, perhaps participating in a pattern in which such speech is common, accepted, expected. But we are appalled when such language reaches out and affects our lives and reputations, shocked that such a thing can happen, truly not seeing that we have contributed to the very situation we now hate. Evil is destructive, messily seeping into a whole system.

So the psalm starts our reflection on the moral ecosphere, a neighborhood where we all live, a place where the deeds of all are recycled and shared back to various shoppers who often cannot avoid them, even if alert to the danger and wishing to skirt it, feeding on actions that are prepared and made available. In fact we scarcely recognize that the deeds offered on the shelves we browse have been produced under circumstances that would make us shudder and recoil if we suddenly saw them, heard them in pursuit of us. Calling into doubt the neat categories of innocent and guilty, non-deserving and complicit, this metaphor recommends us to a suspicion of our own claims. The parable will come by a different route to picture for us roughly the same scenario.

In Luke 16:1-9 we have what is possibly the most difficult of the New Testament parables, due to a frustrating lack of certainty over its particulars. There are so many questions about the referenced practices, so many ambiguous details that even general consensus eludes commentators. Gaps can be semantically productive, but not this many or these particular ones. However, rather than disregard the parable we will read it, making choices where necessary, forbearing to do so if the general sense is clear enough.[2]

> Then Jesus said to the disciples, "There was a rich man who had a manager, and charges were brought to him that this man was squandering his property. So he summoned him and said to him, 'What is this that I hear about you? Give me an accounting of your management, because you cannot be my manager any longer'" (Luke 16:1-2).

We again meet a rich man, a member of the elite of Judean society similar to several other characters in the gospel of Luke. This magnate, as would have been typical, employs a manager who takes responsibility for many of the details of running the estate. The manager is not the rich man's peer but an underling who himself has subordinates over whom he exercises some authority. As the parable opens in the midst of events that have already happened we hear that the manager is accused of something serious—whether correctly or not, from a source of which he may or may not have knowledge, and with or without the opportunity for rebuttal. In telling the parable Jesus does not specify what the hired manager has done, but he does suggest that the deed is serious enough to signal termination of the man's position with this owner at least. The manager does not raise a voice to explain or petition, so we are uncertain of his own sense of the scenario. It is not clear what we are meant to assume from conventions whose key we have lost; a speaker (perhaps

Jesus, but more plausibly the owner) will eventually call this man unjust. But I think in order to appreciate the dynamics here we need to grant this recital considerable moral ambiguity at least in details.

The manager, like the psalmist, is pursued by opponents; those more powerful than himself seem effectively arrayed against him even if they are mostly invisible in Jesus' story. The manager may well have conceived his own evil and dug his own pit, may be faced now with consequences of what he has perpetrated himself. But it is equally possible that he is innocent, falsely accused, too powerless to hope to survive the charge leveled at him suddenly like a flaming arrow shot at a dry house. I suspect we are prone to prejudge him guilty, but he may be less totally in the wrong than we assume. The text does not specify the matter with any precision. Innocence and guilt mingle ambiguously once again. His situation is in any case precarious, though we do not yet hear him allude to it. Before seeing what will be the response of the manager to crisis in his neighborhood let us listen in more detail to the cry of the psalmist from her situation and to the response it generates or fails to find.

The psalmist, in trouble as already noted, appeals for help, pointedly raising the question of innocence and guilt. With a disaster facing her she mingles her appeal for judgment and justice with information about her own deeds and those of her evil-wishers. Her words, noting the hope of help, stress as well its delay in arriving. She speaks of a haven but does so as she races in front of her pursuers. Does the haven receive her? Her imperatives to God, the range of options she offers for divine response, indicate the undecidability of the choice at least for a time: "Save . . . rescue . . . [or] let the enemy hound . . . overtake . . . trample my life." Will God rescue her or not, affirm her claim of innocence or not? If not, why not? In this case God's absence is feared rather than God's presence dreaded, since the speaker is in great need and feels deserving of a response. Is it that simple, we may ask? Does everyone who cries for help expect and deserve it? Is the psalmist as innocent as she feels? Does need translate as right? Does mere crying out testify to sincerity and innocence? Does inaction on the part of the one appealed to signify non-caring, weakness, or perhaps a verdict of guilt? Does it imply partisanship with the others?

> 7　Wake up, Lord!
> 　 Arise and rage
> 　 against my angry foes.
> 　 Provide the justice you demand.

8 Make the world a courtroom
   and take your seat as judge.
9 Then, judge of all the nations,
   give me justice.
   I have done what is right, I am innocent.
10 Put an end to evil,
   uphold the good;
11/12 you test our hearts,
   God of right and truth.
   God who saves the honest
   defends me like a shield.
   God is a zealous judge
   ready to say "guilty" every day
13 if sinners do not turn around (Ps 7:4-13a).

Raising an alternate aspect the psalmist clarifies to whom she is running as she flees from her enemies, from those who attack, prey, tear, hound, overtake, trample, and kill. Now bringing forward explicitly the judicial image, the psalmist delineates the characteristics of the divine judge. Since pursuit is inescapable the question becomes: what response? Having already submitted her claim of innocence, she indicates that she deserves rescue. Given the imagery of hunting developed here she says that rather than her being a shedder of blood, it is her blood that risks being spilled. The point is not to weigh absolute innocence. Her claim is that she has chosen not to be a pursuer even if it means she is pursued. She is substantially, if not totally, innocent of what she is experiencing. A verdict, a rescue will validate her claim, her sense of integrity.

She addresses God the judge and says: adjudicate my claim in this situation. She sees the judge as a helper to herself, to others like her who are pursued by the vicious. If God does the judging well, she insists, moving beyond the possibility of her own complicity, insofar as the system works she will be vindicated and the whole world will witness it. "Make your whole world be the courtroom": we can envision the judge, the plaintiff, the defendants. The psalmist, picturing the scene with us, draws herself as the innocent defendant and imagines the judge, lover of justice, rising from the bench in outrage once the details of the psalmist's situation are clear. Once all claims are weighed—and there is a quick shift to the imagery of smelting metals to separate the valuable from the dross, or to the realm of assaying entrails, perhaps by haruspicy but probably rather the notion of simply testing our decision-making hearts to see what they will do—the just and unjust will stand revealed unmistakably to all watching.

The psalmist's outcry in effect tests God the judge as well, blending her own innocence with the integrity of God: how can God be a judge and such injustice occur? It is a classic reproach. God needs simply to attend, to rouse self a bit, to rise courageously from reverie or inattention, for all to be well. Act as you expect us to act, she prods the judge: provide the justice you demand. Let your own integrity and standards prompt you in my case: this is her request.

At first speaking provisionally ("save me if I am innocent") she now sees the judge as her vindicator, the one to whose side she darts not only when in trouble; perhaps her very relationship to justice has landed her in trouble in the first place. She welcomes judicial scrutiny with confidence, runs toward it with eagerness, offering her self and her deeds for assessment not in the sense that there are no areas for improvement but in the hope of receiving a general validation for her fundamental choices so far. We are, I think, prompted to ask what is it that she has been doing that the unjust are galloping after her? She is not fearful of the judge, does not see him as a fierce old man with a malevolent flashlight. She concludes, unshaken: "I praise God who is right and good; I sing out, 'Lord Most High!'" (Ps 7:18). She evinces virtually no doubt that the system continues to work effectively. Moving from attention to her first cry of innocence we watch her intertwine her justice with that of the divine judge.

But if we are attentive we discover that the response of the judge is startling silence. Clearly pictured as the haven of those in trouble, quick to wade into the fray on their account, virtually unable to avoid giving justice, the judge nonetheless does not exhibit such activity here. The psalmist summarily praises and extols God at the end of the piece, but for a deed that remains hidden from us, verbally at least. Does God respond? how so? Is the appeal enough? Does the psalmist remind herself and others, at the very moment when a deal might seem feasible, where her fundamental loyalties have most consistently lain? Is the psalm more concerned to depict what she will do in trouble than to detail what God will do on her behalf? Or perhaps is her very appeal and her persistence in it God's accomplishment?

Let us switch back to the parable and review the response of the fired manager, reexamine the response of the estate owner to the choices of the manager. The first verdict of the judge is rendered as the parable opens; the manager is pronounced guilty, his fate made verbally clear. But though the decision sounds settled and the manager seems defeated there is an odd delay. Fired orally, the man is left with the keys to the plant, as it were, with access to the company's records, with passwords to the computer systems. And wasting no effort to exonerate himself, explain, or seek some other reprieve, he himself moves on to consider his future. In that small window of time between the announcement of the firing and the enactment of it the manager climbs back into his position of authority to make a few more decisions. Unlike the psalmist, for whatever reason the manager makes no appeal to the estate owner who judges him. It is likely here that the manager is not confident that the scrutiny of the authority will help his case. But like the psalmist, the manager lines up clearly with those on whom he rests his claim for an ongoing relationship once he has lost his manager's job, seeking allies among his peers. In trouble, this man runs from the one giving judgment.

> "Then the manager said to himself, 'What will I do, now that my master is taking the position away from me? I am not strong enough to dig, and I am ashamed to beg. I have decided what to do so that, when I am dismissed as manager, people may welcome me into their homes.' So, summoning his master's debtors one by one, he asked the first, 'How much do you owe my master?' He answered, 'A hundred jugs of olive oil.' He said to him, 'Take your bill, sit down quickly, and make it fifty.' Then he asked another, 'And how much do you owe?' He replied, 'A hundred containers of wheat.' He said to him, 'Take your bill and make it eighty'" (Luke 16:1-7).

We understand from his soliloquizing about his goals and objectives that he knows the crisis is severe, that his employment has been terminated; he is now concerned about what lies ahead. How will he be received? Can he survive once he has been fired from his position? Time is all he has, and not much of that, in order to rearrange his future. He is prompted to his particular action because of a dearth of any but distasteful alternatives, at least as he pictures them. Too weak to hire out as a laborer ("to dig"), he is also too proud to chance remaining unemployed ("to beg"). He needs in some way to carve a living out of the position he is about to lose. Digging and begging, in addition to their specific referents, also comprise a merism. His wasting no breath on self defense, his failure to remark his innocence even in his self-talk may prompt us to doubt it. He goes quickly to the single viable choice he sees. Like the psalmist he wants to survive, and like her he calls for assistance. His appeal is to those he thinks he can count on for support, those who will, from some motive of solidarity, help him out. Whether his allies include those who have accused him to the owner is not clear. He may not know it himself, but he clearly turns to them rather than to the owner. Is his strategy to implicate them, to trap them unawares, to show them that they are only a slip away from the trap they have dug for him?

Unfortunately for us he crafts a crucial part of his decision privately. He announces that it is made without telling us just what it is that will ensure his livelihood once the firing is complete. So we are positioned with the owner's clients and the owner, though lacking their specific frames of reference, as we watch the manager in action. We see a double scene, with the implication of other instances negotiated in a similar way. We learn that he gets the debtors to change the invoices. What we cannot quite pin down is whether such an action is legal or not, whether the beneficiary of the reduced sums is the manager or the owing merchant, whether the newly sacked man is subtracting simply his own commission or his master's profit. The emphasis on haste with the billing records suggests that the manager acts before the firing can be known by the owner's debtors. We understand well enough that part of the manager's motive is his own survival but perhaps some of it is revenge as well. If we assume that the original charge that has occasioned the firing is true, then we can assume as well that subsequent dishonesty would be likely. But if the man has been accused unjustly, works for a harsh man who refuses him any hearing but acts as though allegations were true, then we have another scenario.

What we can discern clearly is a man caught in a net of relationships, a man mingling with some whose innocence or guilt is not clear to us. It may not matter terribly whether he is innocent or guilty; perhaps he is caught in a situation where the moral realities are murky even to him. They are unclear to us, at least as we are reading now. He may have been brought down unjustly by an enemy of his or by an enemy of his master. He feels trapped by what has occurred to him whether he brought it on himself or not. We hear him voice no regrets about the past, simply concerns about the future. He does not, in our hearing, repent of deeds, but he does hope to escape the worst of the consequences. Like the psalmist he may be pursued by someone faster than he is, outgunned by a foe with bigger weapons. In place of appeal is negotiation. He plausibly makes the unwitting cooperation of the debtors the basis of his future, ties their word in with his own. The same ambiguity that attended the judge's response in the psalm is implied here, though at least in the parable we hear something.

Jesus concludes, "'And his master commended the dishonest manager because he had acted shrewdly . . .'" (Luke 16:8a). The manager does his deed, and when it is discovered, in some way we do not witness, all we are told by the parabler, who breaks off the narrative a bit prematurely, is that the owner commends rather than condemns. The magnate appears, praising the shrewdness of his manager rather than challenging his practice. The owner, perhaps in the role of the wicked in the psalm, has to concede that the manager got away with something this time. It is not impossible that the manager is reinstated, though that this parable like so many simply stops rather than concludes suggests that the key points have been offered. The pericope (rather than the parable) ends with advice from Jesus addressed to those listening: a certain such shrewdness is more typical of some than of others, Jesus indicates, contrasting those of "this age" and those "of light."

So we see a pair of texts characterized by environments in which wickedness happens to people. Both the psalm and the parable leave ambiguous—each in its own way—the guilt or innocence of the person threatened. The psalm suggests that the difference comes eventually clear; the parable obscures it. The psalmist's attestation of innocence maintains that she feels innocent; the manager's lack of protestation when accused and fired may mean he is guilty and so does not bother to defend himself, but it may just as well leave us to sense that such words might fall sterile and waste time—time being what he most needs. His moving on to cope is analogous to the psalmist running as she speaks. We probably have more doubts about the manager than about the psalmist, but such a discrepancy is instructive. We hear only the psalmist, not her enemies. Those threatened act to survive, to save their lives if they can do so. The means chosen by each help identify the chooser's sense of situation: the psalmist, beginning with at least the possibility of complicity in wickedness, moves confidently to assert her own innocence and to thank her helper for vindication and assistance; the parable's manager, eschewing appeal to the authority, makes common cause with peers, making them complicit in his guilt if that is what is involved, or in his escape from catastrophe. In both cases the judge seems to affirm the response of the one in trouble, to confirm the efficacy of their choices. The judge does not in either case override the circumstances of danger or fix visibly the situation of wrong. The psalmist seems strengthened in her relationship with the God on whom she has called, as does the estate owner on the man he had thought to fire.

Let us now slide together the parts of this metaphor and see how the ecosystem resembles and describes our moral environment and where it does not seem to fit. Before dismissing what does not fit we will need to consider if in fact the resemblance between the psalmist and the manager may be better than we first sense, since they are morally complex, rather like ourselves: caught in events they did not perpetrate but not necessarily guiltless of other things.

At one level the question of the moral texture of psalmist and manager are not very relevant. To assert total innocence in life situations seems naïve. We may feel innocent of certain things but it is not possible that we are guilt-free in any substantial sense. There is no rock of righteousness for us to own upon which we can crawl to proclaim that we have done nothing wrong, and wait to hear a judge confirm it. The situation of the psalmist is not worked out in detail but she is plausibly not the victim of a random mugging. She is pursued by her enemies for some reason related to her actions. The parable's manager is fired for some situation of which he has been a part, touching him whether he caused it or not. The moral issues and situations are systemic, not punctiliar, involving patterns, not simply discrete actions. Our claims of complete virtue, if we make them, may be sincere but they are short-sighted and incomplete, unreliable.

The more relevant question is the response of the two figures to their situations. They—and we—cope with systemic crisis in what way? The psalmist flees to God in words and presumably in some embodied way as well, offering herself for scrutiny, appealing to the integrity of the judge for her own acquittal. She does not change tack when in trouble, rather remaining committed to choices she has made already. Whatever crisis devolves becomes part of the texture of her life, something she does not cease from doing when evil befalls her. We need not think that fleeing to God means "simply" prayer or liturgy, or that flight involves only running from whatever has caused her trouble. Rather she remains committed to it and begs God to sustain her. I have a friend who from time to time reminds me that she hates the psalms. When I recover enough to query her statement I find that what lies at the base of her aversion is partly that the psalm characters seem fake. In her reading they have problems, complain, get solutions, and boast triumphalistically of them. This friend says she does not know people like that. I agree—but I do not read the characters to be acting so flatly. The psalmist here can be made less abstract if we think of her as someone whose life commitments entangle her in some way with the projects of God and are costing her plenty; as she faces alternatives her options are to back off of the most controversial ones or to stay committed.

The manager actually does something quite similar. He has spent some part of his life span working for someone about to fire him. He, too, has to consider options, which he does, though briefly, in our hearing. Though he does not beg for help from the man who announced his termination, he does cope from within the set of relationships that have composed his life work. In that way he manages to arrange his future. It can be distracting that he seems guilty, at the very least in the assessment of the man who fires him, but it may help if we can look beyond that and see him coping with his situation of evil in much the same way he has already lived his life. Both characters, when threatened, act to survive, to save their lives if they can do so. The means and companionship chosen by each helps identify the chooser's sense of situation. The psalmist links her future to the integrity of the judge and assayer. The estate manager relies on the men who owe money and on the fundamental fairness of the owner. Their actions are fresh chapters in their lives but not new books. Each is both resourceful and reliant upon others, attentive to the limits of self but pushing to do what they can do. We discern a mode of response to a crisis: emergency procedures are called for, but they are not in any case radically different from what one has done before. Recommitting to relationships one has already had, deepening bonds: such things will happen in a crisis. Each character is actually digging in deeper to the commitment already undertaken, granted that the crisis has changed certain things past the character's choosing it.

Key to our working this metaphor is the result of the resourceful action. There is no quick fix, no cosmic authority who can either announce vindication or punishment in such a way that justice occurs. There is no rapid way of altering the many patterns of destruction that are operative in the environment, whether the ecological or the moral (which of course are not so distinct!). Here is where these texts describe us helpfully if we let them. The judge, who the psalmist hints in her appeal may have seemed nodding or inattentive, does not rise up visibly in the text. The owner, weighing in with a compliment, does not intervene to reinstate the manager or even to undo his last administrative action. What then has been accomplished in this ecosystem of relationships? Have these characters gained anything—if not an acquittal, at least a reprieve, an ameliorated situation? How can we catch the fit of the metaphor here?

Each seems satisfied with the result. The psalmist gives thanks for something, which may seem to have passed us by. The manager does not respond to the evaluation of the owner, but presumably can take satisfaction in the fact that his own plans will stand. The psalmist seems strengthened in her relationship with the God on whom she has called, as does the estate manager on the people who have helped him out. It may seem insufficient to us but I wonder if it does not work more effectively to describe our lives than some more dramatic intervention would do. I think we are accustomed to some extent to living in a world where actions have consequences sooner or later, and where the deeds of one may fall onto the head of another as well as bringing down the evildoers. But what we are less sanguine about is the role of God in all of it. In many cases we speak as though we expect God to intervene, to be sure that justice is done visibly, to fix what is wrong, to give us the thing we most want at the moment.

Insofar as we have such an image of God the metaphor of the ecosphere may seem dissonant. The judge figure, the one who weighs the claims of the petitioner, should wake up, rise up, and declare her innocent and rout her foes. We want, I think, to hear that the judge to whom the psalmist has appealed has helped her in some tangible way. Conversely we may be taken aback if we think that the owner of the estate does not step in to fix the altered records, shocked insofar as he seems to approve the deed, and scandalized that Jesus tells such a risky parable. The owner should revoke the lame-duck deeds of the manager. The moral universe should operate better than that, and God ought to be helping justice much more effectively. So we are tempted to find the semantic impertinence of the inactive judge and the condoning owner. Can this be in some way redescriptive of God's ways with us? Or, put differently, in what way might this image cut across what we expect and offer us new insight into God's ways of dealing with us?

The role of the judge and the owner, I think, can shock us into thinking that in at least this particular the metaphor breaks down, does not well describe our situation. The moment of dissonance has to be the apparent passivity of the authority: the silence of God for the psalmist (or at least for us, listening) and the owner's inability or unwillingness to thwart the manager. Why does not the judge fix what is wrong, declare who is guilty and who innocent? By what criteria will the judge act? Is it in response to anything? or to just some things? Does the judge answer only the just? Can the judge ameliorate injustice? The judge does not simply fix things from the outside. Whether the object of hope or the figure to be gotten around, the judge weighs in with approval, not with tangible help. The authority does not intervene, interfere, or act except to permit. The psalmist: is she vindicated, validated, saved? We do not hear her complain. Has she gotten something we missed? We have her praise of God, which is rather generic, perhaps perfunctory. The manager is again silent before the owner: is he punished, rehired? Are the unfair consequences fixed? I cannot read that they are. The metaphor prompts us to reexamine what we expect of God by way of response.

The metaphor pictures our situation, our resourceful and committed appeal, and our going on with our lives. We had better get enough restrengthening from those to whom we turn, however they give it, to keep going at the deeper level to which circumstances have thrust us. We had best be able to live surrounded by opponents visible and invisible, and to continue to cope with them. There is little to be smug or triumphalistic about. The judge is not going to fix what we complain of, is not going to validate our virtue by proving us right about some particular situation. The environment and our own sense of our lives do not envision that.

What the two texts stress is more the integrity of the person trapped and the ultimate inscrutability of God. It may be enough that the psalmist cries out to God, assessing her own claim as she makes it, considering the possibility that she may be implicated in injustice as well as a victim of it. God does not adjudicate directly, but she gives praise for what she has experienced. The manager, his justice ambiguous at least to us, receives a commendation for his action, but we are left uncertain of what happens next in his relationship with the owner. God does not fix what is wrong in the universe. Perhaps in the psalm the pursued eventually does not fully escape those who are after her, or perhaps in the logic of the parable the manager is rehired. Evil may continue to consume since the judge does in some ways seem scarcely to act. The consequences of the deeds done are not necessarily remedied except insofar as the appeal strengthens the hearts of those who have appealed. Perhaps they return stronger to the struggle. Even Jesus, telling the story, does not decry, let alone fix the injustice.

So the texts show well the messy, murky moral atmosphere where actions uncoil from causes and sprawl in one way or another into the lives of all of us. It may happen clearly or not, quickly or not, fairly or not; it may bring a huge and public crisis or a little one, painful in a few lives but not showing up on the larger screen. We are accustomed, I think, to believe that God acted differently in biblical times at least. Indeed at the surface the narratives seem to suggest it. If we read more deeply we may come to reconsider that point. Why does God not help Jesus more? But I wonder if the lives of those who extol God's action and help are really so different from our own. Did they get help that is more tangible than our own? Or did they discern more clearly than we do at most times that the action of appeal, the cry for help, the sort of relationship from which we can continue to ask and to speak is the gift. Our actions, when we have the courage to undertake them, are laced with confidence not so much because God fixes things for us but because we are in relationship with a loving but inscrutable God. Though we might long to hear the judge pronounce in our favor we do not cease being just without it. Choosing to live healthy lives, we are not often dependent on the paramedics. Many aspects of our environmental lives might bear fixing by a super-authority, but the healthful presence in our environment operates in a much more subtle way. The invitation of this metaphor, of these texts, appeals to us to collaborate in as many ways as we can with God at work gently in the ecosystem rather than to pin our fear or even our hopes on the dramatic pronouncement.

NOTES: CHAPTER 6

[1]Wendell Berry, *Sex, Economy, Freedom and Community* (New York: Pantheon, 1992) 25–26.

[2]For a summary of the issues and some assistance with them see Joseph A. Fitzmyer, *The Gospel according to Luke (X–XXIV)* (Garden City, N.Y.: Doubleday, 1983) 1095–1111. One of the key problems on which scholars disagree widely is where the parable proper ends and how far Jesus' commentary on the parable extends.

7

Shepherding:
Psalm 23 and Luke 15:3-7

*H*aving struggled to read and be read by the two relatively difficult metaphors of entitlement-responsiveness and the ecosystem, we may now have the sense of emerging into a clearing as we join the company of shepherds and sheep. Beloved in both testaments, familiar in art, and compatible with our own experience, the metaphor can lead us skillfully to the places where we can rest, healthily if not always comfortably. By their imaginative articulation both the psalm and the parable offer us insight into our relationships with God and with other human beings as we consider the bonds uniting sheep and shepherds. We have in each short narrative the same story of journeying and process of shepherding, simply told from different perspectives: first the sheep's viewpoint, then the shepherd's. Recognizing that the metaphor offers us a way of recognizing, reimagining and then transforming our capacities for this pastoral partnership, let us first quickly review our own experience. As is the case when considering trees and faces, we find the animal metaphor immediately familiar once we stop to bring its many facets to our consciousness.

The easiest place to begin may be our experience in caring for animals, from earliest recollections to the present time. Though we may have this occupation professionally as a veterinarian or a rancher, as a ranger, jockey, or zookeeper, we may also have volunteered to help rescue animals in the face of some emergency or even had the responsibility for caring for a single cat or dog, salamander or snake. The shepherding metaphor stretches flexibly to include many particulars we can consider. We can recall the vulnerability of the animals, perhaps their incapacity to manage survival on their own for one reason or another; their situation of need—for food, care, rescue, or the like—prompts in us a response of pity, a sense of responsibility, a willingness to put ourselves out, to share our resources, to rearrange our own individual priorities.

There is something appealing in the ways animals can engage us, can construct relationships with us, often eliciting something we had not thought or even wanted to extend to them. Puppies may approve of us uninhibitedly, cats pretend aloofness, but in any case we note and respond to their overtures. As parents we allow or encourage children to have animals not only for reasons the children plead but to encourage their nascent fidelity, unselfishness, reliability. So already we can see that animals do something for us as we are offering something to them. We may think about being rescued in some straitened condition by a flask-bearing St. Bernard or watch an elderly person whose friends are dead love an animal. Though we can anticipate or recall situations of abuse when animals become more central than humans or people are much nicer to animals than to colleagues, still the space enlarged by these shepherding experiences is valuable.

The metaphor includes as well the misuse of our position of care. On occasion the weakness of animals seems to invite abuse, their dumbness to allow exploitation. We may also be grieved when the animals let us down in some major way—by destroying our property or by running away. Far from being simply a romantic or soft figure, the shepherding metaphor can be quite bracing, sorting our capacities along a considerable spectrum. Our response to the animals for which we have small or great authority, our ways of exercising and exploring that response, shapes our character.

Relationships with animals also provide significant moments of insight that can be revealing. Having once entertained a fond if unlikely scenario of spending my life on a cattle ranch, I was excited one spring at the opportunity to take a few days' break from teaching Scripture to college students and visit my aunt's sheep ranch in Montana. The snow was deep enough that we slid down the hill to the barns in the early morning darkness, holding onto a rope strung between trees. I had no sooner arrived in the paddock when a group of two-month-old sheep came bounding over to greet me enthusiastically. Flattered and unguardedly gratified, I took a few minutes to notice that what had really drawn them was the rawhide shoelaces in my borrowed boots, which their new little teeth or gums longed to chew. It gave me a chance to think about my own response to what I interpreted as a genuinely un-inhibited and totally joyful response to my mere presence.

I had a similar experience one of the years I lived in a college dormitory. To be hailed by a student as I staggered into the building under my backpack, tired from my long day, was not nearly so gratifying as was the strolling forth of an orphan cat whose dish I had undertaken to buy and fill. I knew that Pilgrim was really issuing a reminder for food rather than a disinterested salutation welcoming me home, but I enjoyed the experience of coming home to a friendly feline encounter. I was often more eager to respond to the cat than to the student's tale of a fight with her roommate or his need for extra time with an assignment.

Experiences such as these are not difficult to recollect once we begin to probe this metaphor of the shepherding process. So we can move on to two texts, and a few other biblical snippets as well, where the biblical sheep and shepherd share their experiences. Let us listen in first to the sheep. She speaks up, as we know, in Psalm 23:

1 The Lord is my shepherd, all that I need,
2 giving me rest in green and pleasant fields,
3 reviving my life by finding fresh water,
    guiding my ways with a shepherd's care.
4 Though I should walk in death's dark valley,
    I fear no evil with you by my side,
    your shepherd's staff comforts me.
5 You spread my table in the sight of my foes,
    anoint my head, my cup runs over;
6 you tend me with love always loyal.
    I dwell with you, Lord, as long as I live (Ps 23:1-6).

We hear her immediately, as though it were the key detail, naming her shepherd: YHWH, the deity whose name, ever since revealed to Moses, signals commitment and fidelity (Exodus 3–4). When Jesus discusses shepherding in chapter 10 of John's gospel he stresses the significance of the shepherd's familiarity with the sheep's names, their responsiveness to the distinctive overtones of his voice calling them. In the psalm we have the sheep alerted to and confident to call the shepherd by the most reverenced of all biblical names. Already we know a good deal about their relationship, since to call God by name is not a simple thing to do.

Nearly simultaneously with her identification of the shepherd she unfolds from the name of YHWH her experience of lacking nothing. The translation before us in fact sets the identification of the shepherd and the experience of all needs fulfilled in apposition to each other. It is a major claim, one we can rethink when we meet the sheep in Luke that lacks, if temporarily, the shepherd himself. The sheep of Psalm 23 does not envision any separation. The experiences she details are familiar to us from many recitations of this psalm: to grassy meadows the shepherd leads her, in them bids her lie down. To restful waters—neither dangerous pools nor uncertain wadis—he guides her, thus enabling her to refresh her parched throat, that is, all the life processes that the slaking of thirst represents. In straight paths, neither too narrow nor too steep, does their journey together proceed.

Sustenance, comfort, security, water to drink that neither sweeps her in nor dries up on her give this sheep and her companions for whom she speaks a sense of ease, justice, confidence. Good food, clean water, time off, health care are the benefits this shepherd offers. She concedes that there are some bad times: walks in dangerous and treacherous places are inevitable; shadows loom above, behind, before. But she is not alone, not lost. The shepherd is there, guiding, reassuring, prodding and supporting with rod and staff by turns as is necessary, silent in this text but his presence felt even when the table is being set.

The angle of address shifts at v. 4b, as the sheep moves from reflecting about the shepherd to speaking to him. And as she does so we get some imagery more extreme than we may have found in verses 1-3, details that seem to strain the metaphor; we also move in closer as we listen to the intimacy of the sheep-shepherd bond.[1] The sheep describes the shepherd as spreading a table for her while her enemies look on, presumably in disappointment, anger, or envy. Commentators suggest the reference may be to leather mats that might protect the sheep from harsh terrain, a possibility not incompatible with other claims the sheep has made but perhaps a little beside the point.[2] He anoints her head with oil, she says, inviting us to consider scenes that range from the salving of ugly and painful injuries to the ceremonial designating of kings. Her cup, or the shepherd's phial, brims, suggesting satiety. The speaker concludes that goodness and kindness, love always loyal, attend and pursue her always. Her dwelling, wherever their journeys may take them, is the presence of the shepherd YHWH who provides all that is needful. Apart from such a shepherd we can scarcely imagine what might happen. This is not a little critter who would do well for long on her own!

The metaphor, familiar from the several places it appears in the Hebrew Bible, is supple in its ability to explore relationships of responsibility and dependence. If the psalm seems over-romanticized to some, per-haps even cloying, the impression may be tempered if we remind our-selves of facets of shepherding it does not mention but that appear elsewhere. The shepherd is most frequently a metaphor for leadership, as we recall in the narratives of the first two kings, chosen in the midst of caring for animals. The young Saul is unsuccessfully in pursuit of lost animals when he encounters Samuel (1 Samuel 8–9); David is shown more successful and effective in his care for sheep at the time of his anointing (1 Samuel 16–17). The prophets broaden the image of the shepherd-leader to describe the scandal of neglect by those with re-sponsibility. Jeremiah 23 describes first the flock as destroyed, scattered, driven away, neglected by the shepherds, and then moves to YHWH's de-termination to fire and replace the negligent shepherds. Ezekiel 34 elab-orates the figure in thirty-one verses, exploring an inversion of the experience between the sheep and shepherd narrated in Psalm 23 be-fore moving more allegorically to sort internecine problems within the flock itself:

> The word of the LORD came to me: Mortal, prophesy against the shep-herds of Israel: prophesy, and say to them—to the shepherds: Thus says the LORD GOD: Ah, you shepherds of Israel who have been feeding your-selves! Should not shepherds feed the sheep? You eat the fat, you clothe yourselves with the wool, you slaughter the fatlings; but you do not feed the sheep. You have not strengthened the weak, you have not healed the sick, you have not bound up the injured, you have not brought back the strayed, you have not sought the lost, but with force and harshness you have ruled them. So they were scattered, because there was no shepherd; and scattered, they became food for all the wild animals. My sheep were scattered, they wandered over all the mountains and on every high hill; my sheep were scattered over all the face of the earth, with no one to search or seek for them" (Ezek 34:1-6).

The responsibility shouldered by one who cares for sheep is spoken of by Jacob when complaining to Laban that as shepherd he has him-self borne the loss of the sheep from his uncle's flock when he might have asserted his non-responsibility for the foraging of wild animals (Gen 31:39). Amos envisions a similar situation in his dreadful reference to the shepherd bringing home only the last fragment of the animal he wrests from the jaws of the animal consuming it (Amos 3:12). The most brilliant parable in the Hebrew Bible, spoken by the prophet Nathan to King David, builds up the picture of a poor family who care for a single lamb, sharing resources with it as though it were one of the family, again in a way similar to Psalm 23. But when another has need of the sheep it is taken as though it were simply a commodity to grace the table of men doing business (2 Sam 12:1-6). David, though guilty of a series of egregious breaches of relationship, is caught by the poignancy of the story, his shepherd's experience rushing to the fore in just the way we are experiencing metaphor drawing it out. Unguarded, indignant, blind, and guilty of the thing he condemns, David at once acknowledges the portrait of non-compassion that his prophet has drawn. The shepherd and sheep metaphor is powerful in its capacity to evoke our experience.

Legal texts reference the lamb as cultic offering, most prominently at the time of the Passover (e.g., Exodus 12) but in other situations as well (Leviticus 1). The passover lamb, itself slain and thus averting the divine slayer from the homes of God's people in Egypt, brings us perhaps most deeply into the heart of the metaphor, the capacity of the weak to serve the needs of the group, the ability of the slaughtered in some way to mediate wholeness and survival. It is a point to which we will return.

But before leaving the Hebrew Bible texts that show us the various aspects of the figure so clearly we need to make explicit to ourselves some slightly different but crucial and apt perspectives that lie implicit in the metaphor. Prophetic castigation of various leaders also reminds us, in case we have forgotten, that shepherding is a livelihood, a way of surviving and providing for one's family and community. Sheep are not household pets. So lying not far beneath even the words of the psalm are the responsibilities of the sheep to the shepherd: the wool, the meat, the fat, the skin all provide subsistence for the shepherd. The shepherd feeds the sheep who in turn feed the shepherd. The reciprocity is clearly implied if not stated directly.

Jesus' parable, drawing on this same general field of shepherding in the challenging physical and economic terrain of the first millennium Levant, tells the story from the shepherd's angle:

> "Which one of you, having a hundred sheep and losing one of them, does not leave the ninety-nine in the wilderness and go after the one that is lost until he finds it? When he has found it, he lays it on his shoulders and rejoices. And when he comes home, he calls together his friends and neighbors, saying to them, 'Rejoice with me, for I have found my sheep that was lost'" (Luke 15:3-6).

Though the details are few, it is not difficult to get a sense of the scene Jesus is setting before us. A shepherd with one hundred sheep is more plausibly an employee than an owner. No matter the degree of responsibility he has been given for the sheep, he is required at day's end to account for all the animals with which he starts. When one is missing he must in some way, and with some risk to them all, go out in search of it. Efforts to diminish or dismiss his risk by indicating that he may well have left his ninety-nine with a partner fail to acknowledge or appreciate the angle we are being given here. A missing sheep opens the shepherd to a charge of irresponsibility or worse. To seek the lost, uncertain of where or when he will find it, unsure where it or he may end up, may not be devoid of incident. But in the parable he finds it and lifts it up onto his own back and shoulders, whether to save it more fatigue, to warm his own body, or simply to hurry the homecoming of all of them. The shepherd's concern changes not to anger, as we might anticipate can follow quickly upon fear, but to joy; his rejoining his friends leads not to complaints but to an invitation to celebration.

These details are not incidental to the Lukan context, not only the general one of the shepherd's journey with the flock to Jerusalem but the specific setting that prefaces the three narratives of Luke 15: authorities are indignant at the sinners' thronging enthusiastically around Jesus and at his welcoming of them.[3] The parable, like the psalm, is more than simply a sweet story; it is an incisive challenge to reconsider the relationship of leaders to people, sinners to God. This parable, like all of them, is not simply a critique but a bold and hopeful invitation to deeper understanding offered by Jesus to those who are unhappy about and resentful of the situation they see. His rhetorical address to them as responsible shepherds (and householders [15:8-10] and fathers [15:11-32]) is not just a gratuitous insult but a provocative invitation. He says, in effect: consider yourself in this role and see if the world all of a sudden looks different to you, and you to it. We, having recently reflected on the whole range of experiences available to us when we have had responsibility for "sheep," can appreciate it as a wonderful moment.

Scholars who have carefully appraised the small differences between the parables as handed on by Luke and Matthew allow us to see some emphases of Luke:[4] In Luke, Jesus angles the parable more directly: "Which of you . . ." is a more personal address than Matthew's "If a shepherd . . ."; it is also bolder to imply—as Luke does—that some of his hearers might have been reduced to shepherding rather than merely to invite them to listen to a scenario removed from their own experience. We may get a similar jolt if someone presupposes some occupation for us that we do not much see as characteristic of ourselves: "When you last collected the garbage in your home town . . . ," or "as you were flipping burgers at the local drive-in . . ." might give us the idea. Or we can ask how we most recently felt when mistaken for a menial if in fact we are a manager. So in Luke's narrative Jesus' intimacy of address is not a frill but a strategy that is potentially distancing or inclusive, depending on the ears of his hearers. Similarly he presses in on the point of responsibility: "Losing one" is not quite the same as saying "one strays," as we can readily sense. The behavior of the shepherd in the Matthew parable is described contingent on his finding the animal: ". . . if he finds it . . ." is not equivalent to the Lukan ". . . when he finds it . . . ."

The gospel of John makes explicit the same set of possibilities that we heard from the prophets. Those who have responsibility for the sheep may exercise it well or betray the trust and exploit the flock. Jesus says:

> "Very truly, I tell you, anyone who does not enter the sheepfold by the gate but climbs in by another way is a thief and a bandit. The one who enters by the gate is the shepherd of the sheep. The gatekeeper opens the gate for him, and the sheep hear his voice. He calls his own sheep by name and leads them out. When he has brought out all his own, he goes ahead of them, and the sheep follow him because they know his voice. They will not follow a stranger, but they will run from him because they do not know the voice of strangers. . . . The thief comes only to steal and kill and destroy. I came that they may have life, and have it abundantly. I am the good shepherd. The good shepherd lays down his life for the sheep. The hired hand, who is not the shepherd and does not own the sheep, sees the wolf coming and leaves the sheep and runs away— and the wolf snatches them and scatters them . . ." (John 10:1-5, 10-12).

Again, as in the Hebrew Bible texts, we sense the metaphor straining as we recognize the differences between caring for animals and for human beings, as well as the fundamental reason shepherds keep sheep. The sheep provide for the shepherd and his family—or for thieves—wool, perhaps occasionally meat, oil, leather. In order for that possibility to remain, the sheep require care and guidance to food, protection from predators, shearing, and so forth. The metaphor, dexterously used in Scripture, highlights the mutuality of the benefit and of the risk. The shepherd and the sheep are mutually dependent—interdependent— though unevenly so. When we hear Jesus suggest in John 10:11 that the shepherd gives up his life for the sheep, at the level of realism it does not make sense. It is the sheep who eventually will be sacrificed for the shepherd; a dead shepherd is of no benefit to the sheep at all, especially if there is danger. A dead shepherd is a failure, unlike slaughtered sheep that provide a series of benefits for the shepherds.

The gospel texts bring us to the same place as do the cultic texts about the lamb of sacrifice in the Hebrew Bible. In fact each gospel has its own way of suggesting a similarity between the Passover lamb and the figure of Jesus: John's last supper is set at the evening of the slaughter of the lambs for the Jewish festival (John 13) and the fourth evangelist links the piercing of Jesus' side, rather than the breaking of his legs, to directions for the slaughter of the Passover animal (John 19:36, cf. Exod 12:46). The synoptics' words of institution at the supper, in some ways more suited to slaughter of sacrifice and splashing of blood than to drinking of libations, offer the same allusion. How is the death of the lamb or of the shepherd able in any way to be a benefit for the flock? How can the metaphor confront us with such an assertion?

So as we slide the worlds evoked by shepherding next to the network of divine-human relationships we find much that fits, and we can isolate what seems odd for further scrutiny momentarily. It is not difficult to see that the whole wide range of relationships of care fits well. Whether we consider the experience of ministering to others or of others meeting our needs, the scriptural texts speak clearly. As indicated above, much of the metaphor will be positive, and we will be able to explore the rich possibilities of growth from responsibility and of surprise from the joys of being cared for. To be parents, teachers, administrators, bishops, baby sitters, overseers is to understand the figure at once, and in detail—the very detail set off in our memories by the details recited by the sheep in Psalm 23 and the shepherd in Luke 15.

But we also have plenty of occasion to consider the negative features of both sides of the figure. To be shepherded poorly by our parents, teachers, administrators, bishops, and baby sitters also gives quick access to the heart of the metaphor. The person who recognizes himself or herself as both shepherd and sheep, probably with mixed success, is doing well with it. Inevitable catastrophes, whether large or small, test and train the shepherd, demonstrate and determine mettle and character. There is no halfway shepherd's role, no such thing as doing a good job until it is too much trouble. The value of the metaphor is all but unsurpassed in its capacities to evoke from us awareness of challenge. We violate our own charge to care for the others undoubtedly, to their sorrow and our own, and we are neglected or abused by those whose role is to care for us. We may single out over-protection or under-care, purposeful neglect or inadvertent acts. We have probably been both violator and victim at some point in our lives. We may understand how apt are intimacy and interdependence for serving as powerful descriptors of the care and responsibility some human beings undertake or are given for each other, as well as the care God has for us, or perhaps as a painful rub if that is not our experience.

We can see, consequently, that the metaphor does not simply describe us as sheep and God as shepherd but rather shows us the process of shepherding sheep or being sheep for a shepherd. It is the relationship that is key, not just the identities themselves. And in a related sense we can infer from the text that the roles are not rigidly fixed. The human being is sometimes sheep but sometimes shepherd, and as the metaphor ramifies in the cultic sections of the Hebrew Bible and in the events around the death of Jesus the role of sheep may be shared by humans but by the divine realm too. Part of what makes this figure complex is the instability of the roles. To recognize oneself simultaneously as shepherd to some, sheep to others is destabilizing. To acknowledge the radical unevenness of the positions, one much more powerful than the other, is also to enter the figure in disconcerting but challenging ways. Possibilities of vulnerability as well as those of abusive power are proffered by the image. The fact that we are not the equal of the deity makes the image a good one, as both our psalm and parable texts bring out well.

But there are a number of places where the metaphor seems poorly constructed to describe our human existence in a helpful way. Which of these dissonances do we quickly discard as pointless, more likely to distract than help us with the value of the metaphor? There are a few instances we might easily dismiss as silly and trivial. No doubt for many animal imagery will never work well. What is endearing and compelling for some so strains reality for others as to be irremediably useless. One of the reasons the Bible is so rich is that it has plenty of options and does not need to force us to swallow what will never be palatable or useful. So even if we can utilize well some of the unrealistic details of the metaphor we will need to be sensitive to those who will not prefer it.

It may be, though, that the very surface inappositeness of the image is what helps it sidle innocently up to us—or allows us to admit it, assuming that any encounter will be painless. We may resemble King David whose self-assessment suggested that he would be just the one to secure justice on behalf of a slain beloved lamb, whereas we can so much more clearly see him as the predator. How can David, who just

before this has adulterously taken the wife of a colleague and then engineered the man's death—at the risk of the rest of the soldiers and the
war effort itself—nominate himself to righteously ameliorate a situation of injustice? Yet such is his sincere and immediate response. He
does not feel threatened by the animal story as the prophet uncoils it.
And yet, as soon as Nathan corrects David's assumption about his own
role the king cannot refuse to see that he has been well described as a
compassionless killer. It is too late for any such denial, the parable having gained too deep an access before the king thought to defend his
own flank. Such is the way of animal stories, of metaphors, of parables.
Our self-importance may well accept revision from this animal image
whether we find such imagery immediately congenial or not.

The metaphor in its various textual elaborations offers us the usual
biblical clarity of contrast between good and evil. We may be tempted
to dismiss the rosy predictions of the psalm and feel aggrieved at the
parabolic straying sheep as well. While we recognize in some ways that
the categories of virtue and vice are not really so discrete and that part
of biblical convention is to discourage well-intentioned indecisiveness,
still the lack of middle figures between these sheep and shepherd extremes may tempt us to dismiss the metaphor. The sheep seem jejune,
excessively naïve. To take seriously the dumb psalmic sheep, so percep-
tive about the services provided by the shepherd, is silly. Worse, her excitement over the table spread before her strikes an almost humorous
note given all we know of the economics of shepherding, of lamb
shanks and flatware. That the sheep has to date experienced nothing
but goodness and kindness is no guarantee that only such lie ahead.

The parable's shepherd seems overly foolish as well, risking the
ninety-nine for the one. Of course we know that the shepherds and
sheep of the texts are merisms, pinpointing extremes within which we
seek more realistic exempla for ourselves. There are various ways of ex-
plaining that facet of the parable away, helping to insure that we do not
suspect the shepherd of irresponsibility or stupidity. But let us reconsider the ninety-nine in light of Luke's context of leadership if not in
the context of our own experience. We can imagine, and only partly
from Luke's setting, the ninety-nine peevishly tapping impatient
hooves, consulting watches, unable to imagine themselves doing anything so silly or selfish as the one whose aimlessness is delaying the return of all the rest. Once again the metaphor may pinch us precisely at
a place of vulnerability. Do the non-straying sheep consider the possibility that they may stray like the one? Have they perhaps already re-

hearsed such a trip, even attempted or managed such an adventure? Or is it simply impossible that they would ever do so? Is the one really different from the ninety-nine?

And do we have the impression from the parable that the shepherd will take the same risk for any of them that is so foolish as to stray, or simply for a few favorites? The waiting sheep are like the elder brother we met in Chapter Three (Luke 15:11-32), not so very different from the boy who goes off to waste "his" money joyously. In that parable, companion to this one in Luke's ordering, the father is as gracious to one son as to the other, granted the differing circumstances. If we feel quite steeped in our virtue, heavily reliable in our dutiful ways, the ninety-nine sheep have a secret to disclose to us. If we can identify with the elder son in the story told in Luke 15:11-32, we need to spend some time pondering the self-righteous bleatings of the ninety-nine sheep, indignant that the shepherd who should be attending to them, rewarding and reinforcing their virtue, is rather wasting time on the one. All of these elements work well to show why the metaphor is so beloved and so effective. What one of us does any of us can do, more or less. Whoever strays, the shepherd will go after us until he finds us.

Similarly the interchangeability of the roles of sheep and shepherd, brought out with particular clarity in the gospels, is an invitation to insight rather than an unproductive oddity. That Jesus is both the shepherd who tends the flock and the sheep whose life is taken for the benefit of the human community is a profound part of the metaphor. That the sheep are vulnerable at one moment and themselves predators at another is also not fortuitous but intrinsic to the figure. The solidarity of the flock and the shepherd as well as the invitation of Jesus to his flock to become shepherds are engaged by this figure. The good of the shepherd and of the sheep eventually become so intertwined that we can hardly sort them out. The two roles are mutually constituting. The shepherd, unlike other hirelings described in John 10, goes to extreme lengths to protect the sheep. If we feel perhaps insulted by being likened to animals as dumb as sheep, and if we do not much care for being assigned the narrative identity of animal keepers, it is worse when the shepherd role turns out to seem senseless as well.

We are back to the irrationality and paradox of the strong becoming vulnerable, the weaker somehow able to gain from the apotheosis of those who ought to have been safe. And yet something like it is a biblical support beam, a central communication of not only the New Testament but of the whole Bible as well. Though we are accustomed, under the guidance of a coherent and rational theology, to think of God as omnipotent and impassible, such is not the consistent testimony of the more diffuse and poetic biblical texts. This shepherding metaphor with all its surface charm brings us to confront the mystery of God who cannot well control or sometimes even influence our hearts, to Jesus who by a number of criteria seems to fail at his ministry. It shows us Jesus himself asking to be spared the ordeal he nonetheless goes through, an ignominious death that fundamentally resembles the cultic experience by which wholeness, health, and holiness are restored so that life can go on in the presence of God.

The instability of the cost-benefit ratio, the uncertainty of the benefactor-beneficiary equation, is a key part of the metaphor. That the lamb both dies and saves, though paradoxical, is asserted in Exodus 12–13. That its blood, draining from it, is nonetheless or thereby perceived as beneficial to individuals within the cultic economy is unmistakable. That the shepherd puts himself out persistently for the sheep who then give their lives for him is key—hence the scandal of the leaders in Ezekiel's and Jeremiah's times who do the very opposite. That the sheep do not understand the big picture is part of what we would rather not reference if we are the sheep! Commentators stress the stupidity of the sheep, their inability to make what we would call decisions. Indeed, some suggest that the very reason the shepherd in Luke carries the sheep on his shoulders is that it would otherwise be too foolish to accompany him home no matter how late the hour. The sheep may have little choice but to rely on the shepherd if it is to survive at all. That there are steps in the relationship that we have not yet experienced does not mean we cannot explore what we do know, recognizing its inevitable incompleteness.

So where does this particular metaphor bring us? We are offered fresh and challenging descriptions of ourselves—and of the others—as sheep, as shepherds, as the straying one, as the ninety-nine more tractable and less needy creatures. The roles we most shrink from are probably the most instructive for us to consider deeply. God is our shepherd, or Jesus is; we are shepherds to and of each other and others shepherd us too, for good and for ill. Jesus is a lamb as well, dependent on shepherds or leaders to protect his life and to provide for it. Both texts stress the totality of the care, but they do so only for a part of the longer story. We know that lambs are slain, and shepherds as well. To be a sheep or even a shepherd is not an exalted existence; rather it lacks status. It is not wholly serene to be a sheep of YHWH, or a shepherd.

What happens when the shepherd gives his life for the sheep or loses it at their hands? Does only one lamb stray, and it just once? Always the same one? Do the ninety-nine learn anything while they wait? The sheep and shepherd coalesce in Jesus and it seems perhaps not to work successfully, if we are honest about it. But what is success? The blend of responsibility and vulnerability may not be a productive one, but what are we producing, or what is being accomplished? What is the "economy" shared by these shepherds and sheep, sustaining and motivating the shepherding process? How does Jesus learn to be a shepherd or a sheep? Does God come through on the promises made to shepherds and sheep through the mouths of the prophets and psalmists: the feeding of the sheep, the seeking of them, their guidance; the shepherd's knowing them, calling out to them, getting them home safely, eventually? "Home safely" is not a place but a relationship into which the shepherding metaphor can draw us deeply, safely.

NOTES: CHAPTER 7

[1]It is entirely possible that the animal image stops here, is dropped by the psalmist who then speaks in his or her own voice. That choice would make better realistic sense. But to continue the metaphor in fact helps us get more from it, so I will presume that the identity of the speaker remains consistent, which is quite compatible with the articulation of the text. A sensitive commentator like Leland Ryken, "Metaphor in the Psalms," *Christianity and Literature* 31 (1982) 16–17, discusses options for construing the imagery, suggesting that the danger is often more that we underread imagery than overread it.

[2]Patrick D. Miller, Jr., *Interpreting the Psalms* (Philadelphia: Fortress, 1986) 116, thinks rather it refers to a line in Psalm 78 that asks "can God set a table?"

[3]Though I have spent little time here on the larger gospel contexts for the parables, having made a different choice for interpretation, the evangelists' skill in showing mutual resonance between parables and their larger narrative matrix is key to investigate. A work like that of Stephen Barton, *The Spirituality of the Gospels* (Peabody, Mass.: Hendrickson, 1992), which explicates the presence of themes like the prominence of joy in the Third Gospel (pp. 74–77), or the importance of conversion (pp. 77–82) helps us catch the significance of points we might otherwise underestimate. For the relationship of parables to their larger contexts see John R. Donahue, S.J., *The Gospel in Parable: Metaphor, Narrative, and Theology in the Synoptic Gospels* (Philadelphia: Fortress, 1988).

[4]Matthew's equivalent parable is in 18:12-14. Kenneth E. Bailey, *Poet and Peasant. A Literary-Cultural Approach to the Parables of Luke* (Grand Rapids: Eerdmans, 1976) 150–153, points out some small but significant differences in the way the evangelists set the parable.

8

The Storehouse:
Psalm 39 and Luke 12:13-21

*O*n a rainy day, or energetic on a sunny Saturday, perhaps in hasty search of some long-vanished but freshly-desired article, we may find ourselves climbing stairs to the attic. Unless we have moved recently or are unusually neat we will find there boxes piled in disarray, dusty albums and envelopes liberated from drawers some time back, jumbled piles of mismatched clothes and shoes. Old toys watch soberly as we come into view and we wonder what they have been up to since we were last on the scene. What is in the room where we keep our treasures? What have we put there, what have we removed, and why? What have we nearly forgotten we have saved, or what have we recently scrapped that we wish now we could find? What memories will be stirred pleasantly for us, and what will we struggle to avoid encountering up here today though we know it, too, lies in wait for us? We can learn a fair amount about ourselves as accumulators as we survey our stuffed storehouses.

And what have we been mumbling, mantram-like, as we ascend the stairs to find what we are seeking? A grievance recently suffered, something unfair that has just happened to us: it need not be large, though it looms almost overpowering in our feelings. We stand accused, misunderstood, blamed, deprived—of resources, position, reputation, confidence. The psalmist says it well with us:

> 2 I said I will not sin!
> I will curb my tongue

and muzzle my mouth
  when the wicked confront me.
3 I kept silent,
  would not say a word,
  yet my anguish grew.
4 It scorched my heart
  and seared my heart
  until I had to speak (Ps 39:2-4).

The resolve to be silent is sincere. Using vivid imagery the poet talks of bridling an animal, or we might say gagging a person about to blurt indiscreetly. The psalmist, ourselves as we mount the attic stairs, vows to store up the injustice, to give it no vent, to allow our opponent no satisfaction: I won't let this get to me; I refuse to make it worse by talking; I know I can push on beyond this episode. But to no avail: like a volcano our heated outrage roils, boils up and over, runs down the sides of our day as our tongue flares into speech. Our resolution collapsed, overleapt like a firebreak, our words are soon off and running out of control.[1]

Luke's gospel specifies just one sample of such a scenario, as though inviting us to supply the many others from our repertoire. He narrates, "Someone in the crowd said to [Jesus], 'Teacher, tell my brother to divide the family inheritance with me.' But [Jesus] said to him, 'Friend, who set me to be a judge or arbitrator over you?' And he said to them, 'Take care! Be on your guard against all kinds of greed; for one's life does not consist in the abundance of possessions'" (Luke 12:13-15). The topos is a familiar one: the reading of the will, a dividing of the property among heirs. How can I be sure I well get enough, get what is mine, what I have coming, what I deserve, need, want? A suspicion, not necessarily unfounded, is that "my brother" will deprive me if he can manage it.

Both texts suggest a grievance beyond the trivial thwarting of our desires, a fear larger than missing some inherited goods. We all live conscious of the possibility that we may not get what we want and need; there may not be enough for me; my rights may not be looked out for. I am suspicious of what is liable to happen. And in this parable as in the psalm, the dreaded event has happened or else the man would not have the need to ask Jesus to intervene in a matter that should be able to be settled without need of assistance from a reliable holy man.

Jesus, as is his wont, picks up the request at the edge and turns it on the empty-handed brother, overrriding the petitioner's request and addressing his condition rather than that of his brother. Be careful you, all of you, Jesus warns, about piling up stuff—real and tangible stuff but other *realia* as well. "Stuff" of whatever denomination is symptomatic of our tendency to be greedy and acquisitive but also of our propensity to upbuild and buttress ourselves. So we, pounding up to our familial attic, may now wonder if we are the threatened heir, may wish quickly to reinventory what our brother and sister are going to claim that should belong to us. The scenario is reminiscent of the story of the father and two sons in Luke 15 but proceeds to explore the details in another way, going down a different section of pathway in the lives of those journeying toward Jerusalem. It seems clear enough that the topic is material possessions, such as are inherited—landed property, most likely. But we suspect that we are also in the presence of a metaphor and should see if we can work with it.

The parable follows:

> "The land of a rich man produced abundantly. And he thought to himself, 'What should I do, for I have no place to store my crops?' Then he said, 'I will do this: I will pull down my barns and build larger ones, and there I will store all my grain and my goods. And I will say to my soul, 'Soul, you have ample goods laid up for many years; relax, eat, drink, be merry'" (Luke 12:16-19).

There is no indication that the wealthy man in the parable references the actual circumstances of the Lukan context—a man who has just died and left at least one son unhappy—but at the very least we get a plausible and helpful scenario for the teaching. A successful landowner leaves not only land but substantial commodities. And Jesus' particular phrasing of the story sketches the features of the deceased all too clearly. Isolated, self-centered, unaware, untouchable—sounding not unlike the judge of Luke 18—the landowner misses a substantial clue dangled by Jesus as he narrates. The land of the already rich man produces well, Jesus says. Farming is not a solitary occupation, nor is even a most skilled owner really able to take credit for the fertility of the soil, for the sun and the rain, for the sprouting and growth of many seeds. Food is not simply a collectible either, in a setting where there will never be a great deal left over beyond local need and where the gross storage by one inevitably deprives others. This aspect of the parable develops the wrongful, unjust stockpiling of goods beyond what we require to the threat or detriment of the legitimate and pressing needs of others, the ignoring of the inevitably communal dimension of food in particular.

But nevertheless, when this particular individual sits down to make his decision about how to cope with largesse he soliloquizes. Framing his consultation as though it were dialogical, he plays all the parts. He refers only to his own situation as though his crops had no cause or effect in relation to others, finding first person singular phrasings adequate to all he needs to say: "'I . . . I . . . my . . . I . . . I . . . my . . . I . . . my . . . my . . . I . . . my'" (vv. 17-19). It is a lot of egotistic isolation for three short verses. We of course might like to interrupt him after he has asked his first question; we can think of options for his goods if his storehouse is already stuffed full. It is not rare or difficult to feel indignant when he quickly decides storage expansion is the most likely solution—indeed the only one we hear him contemplate. We are disgusted as he envisions climbing triumphantly onto the big pile of grain, sitting at ease on the comfortable verandah of his superbarn. And when he addresses himself, clapping himself affectionately and approvingly on the shoulder and advising some time off, he seems additionally grotesque. We may wonder if the man who thinks to consult no one will have much of a vacation, even should he feel at ease to take it.

Depending on our reading circumstances and partners our indignation may be short-lived and short-circuited, since many will point out that the sentences describe our whole capital-obsessed and resource-consuming Western culture all too clearly. When I taught courses on Gandhian nonviolence the subject of the Mahatma's vegetarianism inevitably arose. Gandhi was a great experimenter and obsessively interested in the human body's intake and outflow of food. Famous for his fasts, he also loved to select a few dates or a gill of goat milk or some small portion of lentils for his frugal meals. Students pointed out correctly that he was fussy about eating, and demanding in his way—obsessive is indeed a fitting word. But, though agreeing, I would point out that if Gandhi were to visit any of our supermarkets he would find our common (and probably most of our individual) obsessions with food choices more startling than his own. So while we may harrumph and point disdainfully to the "rich fool" as he is called in gospel parlance, there may be a number of people standing behind our large barn-hugging selves, gesturing demonstratively at us.

The psalm in any case offers us a soliloquy as well. When we last left the aggrieved psalmist an emotional and verbal fire had ignited and the opponent was getting scorched. I think that explosion occurs for this psalm offstage, as it were. There are numerous psalmic occasions where we hear torrents of indignant detailed complaint or accusation, but not here. The person whose prayer we have joined is now past the outburst, unheard by us perhaps since we know the typical content all too well, having many such incendiary storehouses of our own; the fire has burned itself out and he or she now turns to God:

> 5 Lord, what will become of me?
>   How long will I live?
>   Let me see how short my life is!
> 6 You give me a brief span of time;
>   before you, my days are nothing.
>   People are but a breath:
> 7 they walk like shadows;
>   their efforts amount to nothing;
>   they hoard, but others gain (Ps 39:5-7).

Much more polite and clearly feeling more desperate than the character in Jesus' parable, this individual is actually concerned for the same thing, which is the metaphor that we are examining. The point of the prayer is that if only we can know how much we are going to need—how many days, what size of life—we can plan sensibly and not run out of what we require. Life is feeling brief to the person uttering this prayer, or perhaps overlong for the resources allocated to cover the span. The suitcases are out on the bed; the question is what to pack that will suffice. The man or woman who speaks this prayer asks for the blueprint, the calendar with not the first but the last day circled so that plans can be made. The words about days narrow and few, life evanescent as vapor, our earthy selves going about like mere shadows all testify not so much to literal shortness of span but to our sense of vulnerability. Little is doable but we feel the need to know how to allocate our miserly portion lest we run short.

There used to be, in the early days of television, a program whose name escapes my memory. Some readers will recall it. By some process or criteria a few women from the studio audience would be acclaimed winners and eventually invited for some tiny amount of time to rush around amid consumer items and drag the most desirable ones into their territory, thus securing them. Petite women would strain to embrace "Frigidaires" in slow dances over to the sidelines, would attempt to fill their arms with more toys than they could possibly balance, all to the frantic and encouraging cheers of their friends in the live audience of the day. (I must admit to once playing a rather similar children's version of the same grab where with no doubt a smaller viewing audience we could bid for unquestionably smaller prizes with potato chip bags.) The program was not intrinsically bad, and I am sure the triumphant winners took good care of the items they managed to amass and claim. But the process of the program sticks in my mind as an obscene parody of what we may be tempted to do with our human span. It is a race not limited only to the frenetic types we might see in the trading pit on Wall Street or the conspicuous consumers in Hollywood's Rodeo Drive boutiques. We all long to stuff our storehouses. The metaphor under consideration invites us to recognize it so we can go on from there.

So what we can see is lined up across a spectrum. Some goods—or "bads"—accumulate that we wish were not there: resentments, fears, slights, angers, grudges. And we pile up other sorts of goods unjustly, excessively, thoughtlessly, wastefully, cloyingly. The process of storing overtakes us. The storehouse entraps, closes up on us, closes us in, shuts others out. The "stuff" pushes us off into nooks and crannies, stores us high and out of reach of those in need. Our accumulation thrusts itself forward in place of ourselves to meet any inquirers. I become my clothes, my role, my degrees, my bank balance, my classy address, my curriculum vitae. Rarely is happy equilibrium achieved. There must be more to be acquired.

What we heap up may outlast our needs as seems to be the case in the parable. The question of who will inherit is almost a stock question in Scripture. But when we reflect on the storehouse as a metaphor rather than a literal barn I think we can see the fear of diminishment as well. What is it that we need for our lives: surely some security, some esteem, some affection, some relationships. Those, as I think we can readily agree and see on every page of the Bible, are good and desirable. We do heap up: that is our way and there is little point in denying it. Pondering our common propensity, I suggest that it is related to our corporeality. We, like birds and squirrels and unlike rocks and stars, must keep replenishing because we consume. We continue to eat because our bodies convert former meals to energy and waste. The drive in us to get a little ahead has to be deep and ingrained and the fear of running out very primal. The issue Jesus fingers, and the psalmist too, is how much is too little, what is enough, or too much? Of course it depends on what commodities we have chosen to store. What do we heap up, fearing who will gather it from us—before we move on or after? What precious metal reserves are backing up our stacked currency? How much reputation do we need, how much approval? What are we willing to do to gain it—not even what dishonesties will we endure to look good to others, but how central in our life journeys is the climbing of the ladder of public esteem, however private some of our "publics" may be?

I think it is all too easy to see where this metaphor fits our experience and that of people whose lives we observe; and we can, as readily, strip away what seems not to fit. The man in the parable is obscene. Our storehouses are much smaller and fewer. Perhaps sheer scale can disqualify parts of this metaphor for us. As usual the most valuable aspect may be the moment of surprise, the recognition that the storehouse itself is a given, the process of storage inevitable. We are not advised simply not to store up but redirected to a deeper search. We begin to see that the storehouse is not a thoroughly negative image. It is a matter of making good decisions about what and how we store, insofar as we are able to manage by rational decision.

When we haul ourselves up to the attic or dash down to the basement to look around, on what scale are we doing our assessing? What angers, grudges, denials do we have stored up, not quite forgotten if not necessarily lying near the front of the place? What have we most carefully and consciously stored; what do we take most care to protect from marauders: perhaps it is material, but often it is a less tangible role or conceit about ourselves that we most treasure. Do we greedily number our grudges at our family and friends? enjoy the photo album of people we have surpassed in our cleverness? What do we seldom use, what have we genuinely outgrown that we could toss away, recycle, mulch? Why is there so much junk that we have little space for things we genuinely value more? Can we envision a smaller storehouse—not *no* storehouse—at least for some of our treasures? Which of our stored possessions are incompatible with which others? Why are we saving them all? Material goods are part of the problem, to be sure; the phrasing of the parable makes that undeniable. But Jesus is concerned about greed in all its forms and in its root insatiability; he invites us to take a look at it, as does the psalm. It continues:

> 8 Why do I wait for you, Lord?
>   You are my hope
> 9 to save me from my sins;
>   do not make a fool of me.
> 10 I will keep quiet.
>   I have said enough,
>   since all this is your doing.
> 11 Stop tormenting me;
>   you strike and I grow weak.

12 You rebuke us for our sin,
    eat up our riches like a moth;
    we are but a breath (Ps 39:8-12).

The psalmist invites us now to consider two further points. He, or she, cries out to God that if intentions can be counted, all is well. There is nothing to await or expect—to fasten one's hope upon—outside of God. The one praying these verses is not simply saying that all roads lead to heaven, since the concept of the afterlife or eternity spent in God's presence is not a central characteristic of Hebrew Bible spirituality. We ourselves, able to envision an afterlife that includes an ongoing relationship with God, may utter a similar sentence, all the while continuing to stock our storehouse. We cannot think to have God rather than material goods, self-esteem, good friends, and so forth. God does not replace those things in our corporeal existence. But neither do those things take the place of God. We pray to be spared the scorn of the fool, perhaps the one who set off our tirade regretted by the end of v. 3. What the psalmist invites us to consider deeply here is once again the storehouse: not will we have one, since we will; but what is in it? How are the things of God to be arranged and stocked? Who is at work in our storehouse besides ourselves? And if the storehouse cannot very safely preserve inconcinnities—water or acid with paper goods, angry memories with compassionate impulses—we push on to consider the question of compatibles.

Since the storehouse is a spatial image, can be envisioned as a building, has come to be recognizable as the place where we live, we can imagine it as our home. When people place their homes on the market in hopes of selling them the realtors often schedule open house afternoons. The owners are typically asked to vacate the premises for a few hours so that others can browse freely, comment uninhibitedly, ask frankly. The stuffed storehouse metaphor as worked in both psalm and parable invites us to suppose just such a scenario. We as owners step out temporarily and others come in. We, however, sneak back in and mingle invisibly—perhaps in disguise—and are undoubtedly quite startled to hear our goods discussed. What we thought would be the envy of all is perhaps disregarded or denigrated. What we have grown so accustomed to as scarcely to notice, others remark enthusiastically. We may be surprised at what others wish to remove in their so much greater need, to our shame that we were so unaware. The exercise will be instructive, this matter of reassessing our stored goods.

The question becomes all the more pressing as these lines of the psalm move ahead with a rather shocking and rarely emphasized image: the divine moth.[2] The psalmist, having already given up the project of blaming the invisible enemy, the wicked of v. 1, reveals now the real adversary by addressing God. "All this is your doing . . . . You . . . eat up our riches like a moth" (vv. 10-12). What is more dreaded in our closet of stored woolens than the sight of the fluttering moth? Here the moth has the run of the storehouse, access to our most guarded treasures, and delights in reducing them to gaps and edges, trellises and trestles. It is a bold image, one of the best small metaphors for God. Which of our treasures is attractive to the moth? vulnerable to the moth? From our perspective the moth is destructive of our piled-up goods. But moths have their reasons, their agendas that may have little to do directly with thwarting us. What is the quality of our distress when our inflated ego becomes moth-eaten, our pride in our achievements begins to appear worn even to ourselves? If we miss a rung on the ladder of success in our field, if someone overlooks or underrates our importance, will we survive?

Again it is crucial to recall that we are in the hands of a metaphor, not a video. The biblical voices tend to sound as though they envision God as very powerful in their lives, intervening directly, punishing personally, rewarding on a piecemeal basis. It is a facet of God and of language about God that we explored in Chapters 5 and 6 with our reflections on entitlement and the environment. It may be that the ancients' sense of the matter was that God did function in just that way, but for me, at least, it is not so simple a cause-effect transaction. God does not, in my view of it, plan the universe in order to recompense our human choices directly. God is not maliciously nibbling away at just the very things I love best so as to punish and thwart me. The common moth, also known as *tinea pellionella*, is not a name for God getting back at me for my excesses but rather my opportunity to converge my relationship with God and other creatures with my hopes and fears about the storehouse. It is a way of naming the great fear of diminishment, of inadequacy. The moth has as parents some of my fears about God and some unaccepted feelings about my own worst scenarios. But it also implies the possibility of negotiation over my treasures, of revaluing some of them. The moth opens up the option of a relationship. I am not in the attic by myself, much though I might wish it so and often though I might feel it to be so.

When we lose our possessions by theft or fire, earthquake or storm, can we go on without at least some of them? The moth encompasses all of these possibilities and many more. Might the journey even be easier when we are not carrying so much? Might we choose another path if we are not so laden, or if we are more healthily provisioned? If we cannot seem to manage without a full complement of status, approval, popularity, and goods, cannot bear being misjudged or misclassified occasionally by those who watch the inventory over our shoulder as it accumulates—what does the moth do for us then?

The parable ends with the arrival of the supermoth: "But God said to [the rich landowner], 'You fool! This very night your life is being demanded of you. And the things you have prepared, whose will they be?'" (Luke 12:20). The moment will come to all sooner or later; avoiding it is clearly not the point. The man in the parable, unlike the psalmist, has not even thought ahead to ask for the horarium. In fact he has already announced to himself, unlike the psalmist, that there are many years ahead. Counting his time in cubic yards of grain, presuming that his life—like his grain and his barns—is indeed his to manage, he makes a fatal error. Unlike the psalmist who wants to know how few suitcases he or she can stock from the items in storage, hoping to ration out the choices to match the exigencies, the rich landowner orders steamer trunks to fit his stored up goods. And God, perhaps having tried to nibble earlier, weighs in with the crucial insight for the man: it is not just *"your* life," and I who have shared some generously out to you am choosing this moment to reel it in.

And the recurrent question—how do the goods get passed on—that triggered the parable and punctuated the psalm (v. 6) has now become a much deeper matter. Jesus, speaking God's deathbed-side words here, is not interested simply in the process of inheritance or even in the important justice-rooted question of redistribution of grain to hungry villagers, excess land to the landless. However will this man, or will we, go forward, so gross and inflated with obsessive acquisitiveness? His engorged self, just so recently encouraged solipsistically to take life easy, is now being told by another to take it very seriously. Where is his supple and genuine self as he waddles forward, longing perhaps now to jettison some of what he has piled up but finding himself unable to do so? His few handbreadths are labored, his insubstantial shadow vanished amid the stuff he has placed around it. He has become his barns and now finds them inadequate, or perhaps we do. Our storehouses are us. And so what is our life's accumulation?

Part of what is jarring in this short text is that there seems no warning. The man has no sooner retired than the axe falls. We all know of similar cases. But the psalmist would suggest (and the parables too) that there is indeed warning. The little moth has fluttered around quite a bit in its irritating and inconvenient way before the larger one arrives. What has the man been doing, whom has he been heeding or not hearing, that he has finally to be called so abruptly? And though this seems an unlikely observation, given the plain sense and the history of interpretation of the text, are we so sure the man dies at the announcement of it? The parables tend to break off unfinished, to stop *in medias res.* There is more to life than food, we are advised by our parabler on another occasion. The man is asked to bring forward his life, and he is given a serious question to ponder. He does not answer, for whatever reason. Perhaps he dies; perhaps he is trying to search for something stored back very far, piled up very high, buried almost too deep. And we are given a moment for reflection as well.

The man is speechless in the parable. Perhaps if we can switch back to the psalm a final time we can offer him—and ourselves—a response that is timely for at least some of us:

> 13 Lord, hear my prayer,
>   my cry for help.
>   do not ignore my tears,
>   as if I were alien to you,
>   a stranger like my ancestors.
> 14 Stop looking so hard at me,
>   allow me a little joy
>   before I am no more (Ps 39:13-14).

We beg God to listen, to keep listening, not to turn away no matter what we have said. Those in straits call to God and expect it never to be too late. If God's ear gives in, if we get a reprieve, a gift nibble from a monitory moth, then there is hope for those who hope in God. The landowner may come to acknowledge with the psalmist that he is only—happily—a passing guest with no need for huge barns. A sojourner like his people, he now reclaims solidarity with them. A backpack may replace our steamer trunk. Such a person, like an "illegal alien," has no secure rights, no privileges, nothing entitled. He waves the moth away, the ear he has just poured his plea into. Better with you at a distance, he seems to say: my storehouse is fragile, flimsy, appropriately so. I have stripped it down to the bare essentials. Ease up now for a time. Let me get accustomed to what is there. God is an unreliable guest there, liable to behave in ways uncomfortable to us who like to pile up treasures.

Visited by the moth, we claim the right to restock in private. The moth will no doubt be back for a look soon enough.

The person of intimate faith, bold enough to call God a predator, eager enough to pour words of both anger and pleading into God's face, may in fact not be as averse as it sounds to having God around. Will God in fact decamp? for long? for good? I think we can hope and trust not, whatever we may say when harassed. God, patient, irritating, hovering, eyeing interestedly treasures we may not need, will not be absent long, I think.

NOTES: CHAPTER 8

[1]Commentaries on the psalms, in my view, are of limited use for the sort of readings offered here. Though there are some instances where psalm commentaries illuminate useful detail, a work like G. B. Caird, *The Language and Imagery of the Bible* (London: Duckworth, 1982) is much more creative in helping cue us to the value of tiny details in psalmic language. See, for example, his discussion of levels of intentionality (pp. 37–61) and his points about ambiguity (pp. 109–121) for practical pointers about reading metaphor.

[2]A tiny metaphor like the moth can provide a good occasion to begin exploring a challenging work like Peter W. Macky's *The Centrality of Metaphor to Biblical Thought: A Method for Interpretation of the Bible* (Lewiston, N.Y.: Edwin Mellen Biblical Press, 1990). His patient sorting of the many issues of metaphor offers access to good reading practices.

9

The Other Side:
Psalm 41 and Luke 10:25-37

*F*inally we come to a figure less obvious than tree, storehouse, and shepherd, though simpler to approach than we may have found entitlement and ecosphere. But the metaphor of the other side is, like the others we have examined, capable of generating significant insight as we explore its workings within a pair of texts. Its rather generic or noncommittal phrasing can help us sort freely through our imaginations and memories to locate a good place of access. What is our experience of the other side and what can it show us about where we are standing, where we see others positioned, and where we wish to direct our journeys—or let them be directed?

We may, when reading the newspaper or watching the news, be surprised at what soccer fans of one nation can do when they are guests in the home stadium of "the other side." There are neighborhoods in which we feel very uncomfortable if we find ourselves lost there or passing through at night. Or sometimes we can come upon desolate places where people drop off their garbage, bring old appliances, abandon aging cars, store hazardous waste; the dump is out of their daily range, not near the place where they will need to look or live, though others may dwell nearer. Borders mark the one side from the other, processing us through little gatehouses, checkpoints, or lonely stretches of barbed wire to become intruders or citizens, aliens or guests. School children map out safe spaces—sections of school benches, places in the yard, social networks, even colors—where they are comfortable and from which they can exclude others, confining them to the other side. We may even have had friends who cease being such when they do something that puts them beyond our sympathy and our ability to accept peacefully; we or they end up consigned to the other side. Race, ethnicity, and gender can start us on one side or another, and wherever we may stand, the others can seem intimidating, strange, off-limits, unimaginable. Like the storing up of goods of all kinds, the process we considered when investigating the storehouse, the drawing of sides is almost inescapable, given our human condition. We may not be able to stop taking sides but we can perhaps recognize more clearly what we are doing and make some of our choices better.

To explore this metaphor we will start with Luke's gospel. While the journeyers—Jesus and companions—are on the way to Jerusalem an expert in the Law asks a question of Jesus, to test him, Luke asserts. The notation that the question is a test instructs us to read with such a convention in mind, not that there are not many other reasons to ask questions. Testing is not inevitably negative though the gospels tend to focus on the pejorative and malevolent when describing or setting up encounters between Jesus and many of his interlocutors, authorities in particular. Any question, whatever the asker's intent may be, reveals a good deal about the dynamic between speakers. As before, we are invited to participate in the exchange: to test the adequacy of question, response, reactions, to find out where we stand.

In this case an expert in the Law asks about inheritance, that popular topic of the travel narrative: "'Teacher, . . . what must I do to inherit eternal life?'" (Luke 10:25). To inherit is to come by some entitlement into possession of something. The most common way perhaps, in our experience, is to be an heir related by blood or by some other intimate tie—marriage, close friendship, a long work relationship. Additionally, however, there has to be some assessment by a duly constituted authority that, of the many who could wish or claim to inherit, one is particularly and explicitly entitled to do so. In the parables involving inheritance that we have examined (though this present passage precedes the others in Luke's order) one son seems to find it difficult to get some of the property of their father away from his brother (Luke 12:12-21) and two sons want to inherit but find it difficult while their father still lives (Luke 15:11-32). Inheritance is often far from automatic.

To lay claim to eternal life, of course, is not quite the same as inheriting tangible goods. We recognize that the questioner employs a metaphor to talk about what he hopes to gain. The lawyer's question implies that, rather than surviving another, he himself will need to die. But the eternal life that he wishes to enjoy is not precisely nor most properly to be thought of as a matter of entitlement. That the lawyer makes the first accommodation in stride is probably a safe assumption. His death will necessarily come first. But whether he is literal or metaphorical about the question of inheriting the hereafter, and by some affirmed and reliable entitlement or on the basis of some relationship, is not clear. Hence our invitation to consider the possibilities as we see them. Whether the lawyer intends to ask how he can corner eternal life so as to deserve it or whether he is asking something slightly different, we may consider both questions since they are implicit in the figure he uses.

Since Luke has said that the man is posing a test we need to examine what it might be, whether it is a trap designed to bring down prey or an assay constructed to find a sensible response. The gaps in the question—uncertainties that Jesus, insofar as he answers, will need to construe—are at least four, involving what/I/must do to inherit/eternal life. Let us sort each of these a little farther. Is there a "what" for me to do, something clear and manageable? Am I most accurately the one who does it, or is it at least partly collaborative? Is my action directly linked to my inheriting, so that if I do my part my reward will be certain? And is eternal life such that we can envision it as heritable? Theoretically as he assembles a coherence from the parts of this question Jesus has to choose one or another construction of the issues proposed. Insofar as Jesus himself is being judged he will answer well or not, depending on criteria the lawyer sets up. We shall see in time that though the man proposes to test Jesus, Jesus manages to compose a different view of the matter and to test his questioner: to help him cross to the other side.

Any attentive gospel reader will have long recognized that Jesus often prefers not to take questions as they have been posed. In all the gospels he tends to field queries, regrasp them and then toss them back so that he can discuss the relevant matters that seem most urgent to him, whether those are the topics initiated or not. It is one of his most persistent character traits, and a very revealing one in virtually every instance. Here, though he is offered a long court in which to make his response, we may be a bit surprised to see that he taps the question back just beyond the net, making his questioner run quickly forward to regain control. To the question and questioner Jesus replies, "'What is written in the law? What do you read there?'" (Luke 10:26). As anticipated, Jesus suggests that the Law is the place to start the search and he metaphorically pushes "the book" back toward the man with the suggestion: look it up and read it out.

Of course it is not so simple since "the Law" is vast and complex, written and unwritten, ancient custom and the inevitable contemporary interpretation accruing and mixing as life evolves. Even if we assert that the expectation of and quest for an afterlife is relatively new to Judaism at the time of Jesus, the question of how to line up for it remains coextensive with how to live the life we are in the midst of now. Contrary to what we so often hear or assume, the land symbolism of Deuteronomy, the worldview underlying the cultic procedures, the justice challenges and critiques of the prophets, the secular-sounding wisdom quest and the stark options of apocalyptic all invite a complex and multifaceted ethical living. The accumulated heritage of Judaism on the question of how to spend a life gainfully is abundant. So though Jesus signals clearly enough that he is not going to start to search within the huge tradition, his invitation to the lawyer that he should get his investigation started himself is not necessarily dismissive. Jesus has been cautious with the question, evidently not willing to be drawn too far without more information. Or, to put it a bit differently, he may not yet be certain of how he can best respond to the question being asked, most benefit the man inquiring. On key and unfocused questions such as this one it is a move of his with which we are familiar.

The man does not hesitate, at least as Luke unfolds the scene to us, to proffer his response, his opinion, answering, "'You shall love the Lord your God with all your heart, and with all your soul, and with all your strength, and with all your mind; and your neighbor as yourself'" (Luke 10:27). It is, of course, a beautiful and apt answer, a view Jesus approves elsewhere and even articulates himself while discussing important truths.[1] The two sentences are arguably the core of Judaism, of Christianity, of Buddhism *(mutatis mutandis),* of many ethical systems, perhaps of the quest for fullest humanization. It is difficult to imagine improving upon what the lawyer has stated. Nor does Jesus revise the answer: in fact he validates it, though he does alter the question. Jesus responds, "Do this, and you will live" (Luke 10:28). "Live" is not the same as "inherit eternal life." Jesus, preferring the answer to the question, suggests that a certain way of living now is compatible with a certain way of living later. The challenge from the Law, succinct though it is, takes the lawyer and all of us past envisioning a tidy "what," encourages us to abandon projects that are restricted to "must do." Once we are engaged fully with the challenge of these two legal "snippets" our struggles may diminish thoughts about rewards. Loving God deeply, comprehensively, and consistently, and putting others on the same side as ourselves or ourselves on their side is not easy to "do."

We may by now suspect that the man testing is himself being tested and found a bit crass or naïve. Jesus is not yet exposing much of his own viewpoint for whatever treatment the lawyer may have in mind to do. It does not appear that the man soon learns anything he does not already know. Jesus avoids saying anything controversial, taking a stance that might be easy to contradict or contravene. The clearest gain is that the metaphor of inheritance vanishes from the equation. That choice of phrasing so far is the clearest indication of Jesus' thinking. The lawyer, not wholly satisfied, not in any clear way taking the point, presses on. The Lukan narrator, attributing a motive again, says, "But wanting to justify himself, he asked Jesus, 'And who is my neighbor?'" (Luke 10:29).

Again the question exegetes the questioner. "Who is my neighbor" sounds similar to "What must I do". The motivation assigned to the question suggests that the lawyer does note or sense that Jesus' cryptic responses somehow put him in the wrong, on the other side. Whether it is the teacher's refusal to be drawn, his implied correction of the question proffered, or perhaps something nonverbal in the encounter, the result is that the man feels the need to regain status. Social scientific critics, alerting us to some of the cultural dynamics of the scene, show how such ripostes work.[2] Honor is an almost tangible public commodity, not simply a personal or private feeling. If the lawyer challenges Jesus verbally in public Jesus must offer back some sort of a rejoinder, since not only his own honor but God's also is at stake. The lawyer moves then to counter with his own fresh challenge, and so they contend until it is clear who has bested whom in the exchange and whose shame is unavoidable. Though our late twentieth-century categories may be slightly different the genre of question and answer, thrust and parry, is not unfamiliar, and we can sense the embarrassment that comes with a put-down, if that is not too strong a descriptor for what Jesus does here; we can imagine the flinch from the questioner who lands clumsily on one foot when expecting to settle gracefully on two.

To return to our spatial metaphor: the lawyer feels that he is being dumped down unceremoniously in an undesirable spot and scrambles to his feet again, hoping to gain access to a more congenial place. He deserves better; he is smarter than he looks, more deft than he feels. One way of moving is to trade places, to pull his opponent down as he rises to his feet. So he asks a question, this time even less to inquire for new insight but more to reposition himself as right. The response he draws from Jesus this time suits perfectly the project upon which the man is embarked: getting safely up onto the other side. We, poised with him to understand the metaphor, are about to go on—be taken along on—a journey.

So Jesus replies to the man's latest question but picks up his first as well:

> "A man was going down from Jerusalem to Jericho, and fell into the hands of robbers, who stripped him, beat him, and went away, leaving him half dead. Now by chance a priest was going down that road; and when he saw him, he passed by on the other side. So likewise a Levite, when he came to the place and saw him, passed by on the other side" (Luke 10:30-32).

A narrative this time rather than a brace of apodictic laws, aimed in some way we must discern, is offered in response to the question of how to live for eternal life and who is neighbor. And in the context of Luke's extended travel narrative Jesus offers here his own miniature journey story, though with the direction reversed. Jesus, en route to Jerusalem via Jericho, describes a set of journeys coming the other way. Though the first traveler's gender is given minimally, the person is otherwise tagless. It seems not to matter whether he is Jewish or Gentile, rich or poor, landowner or trader, kind or mean, moral or immoral. It is difficult to imagine knowing less about a human being than we do here. What brings the man to Jerusalem and back along the dangerous Jericho road also remains opaque.

But of course the man does have a little more to lose—his footing, his clothing and other property, his physical health, nearly his life. All that we really need to focus upon is his barely fluttering ribcage and his position at the side of the road. He appears headed for the eternal life under discussion between Jesus and the lawyer. To leave someone half dead may imply that those going off with the man's possessions think him dead or on the verge of it. His breath and his position on the road are all that define him, perhaps his feet and ankles sticking out from some obstruction that might otherwise conceal him completely. The robbers, we may also note as they leave the scene, are all but invisible. Jesus, telling the story, does not pause to excoriate them. They go off, even more insubstantial than the man they have left for us to examine insofar as we may choose to do so. The heap of human being, almost utterly generic, has no claim on us that we should take a look: perhaps the contrary.

That far from inviting something from us, the next thing we are shown is that the beaten person repels it. The priest and Levite are relatively familiar to us from other contexts. All Jesus chooses to suggest here is that the two passersby have roles and responsibilities in their society. Though much has been written about their identities and positions such details are almost red herrings here. As we discovered when considering the Pharisee and toll collector, labels help us briefly but not for long; and they may distract us if we become too tangled in stereotypes. The priest, like the beaten man, is going down from Jerusalem. Why he is journeying, what he has been doing or where he is headed, what his obligations may be when he arrives—none of the detail is fleshed out. We can make some assumptions, pose some conventional understandings against the scene. But I think his actions are the most significant: he sees the man and passes by on the other side. The Levite is not dissimilar. Whatever direction he is heading, he glimpses the body and also continues to move along on the other side. The repetition suggests that the positions of the three are what is key: two on one side, one on the other.

Since we are alert to the tremendous power of our own experience here, let us stop and review it. It is difficult to imagine anyone from among our contemporaries not readily identifying with all three characters visible in the scene so far. Being set upon by robbers is a situation we can imagine with a hundred grim variations. Becoming the next victim while attempting to assist a person in distress is all too common. The very vulnerability of the one lying at the side of the road poses a vivid reminder of what is lurking in wait for us if we slow or stop, or choices we might be willing to risk on our own might involve our families in resulting catastrophe, so they become less feasible. What will our dependents do if we are beaten and robbed, if we are infected or sued, kidnapped or murdered? The positioned stranger reminds us of the classic "pigeon drop": the fat purse lying temptingly in the alley, drawn back by an invisible string as we come closer to examine it. We know of too many attacks on motorists who stop to assist fellow travelers ostensibly in distress. Poor people grab the wallets of those who foolishly take them out to make a kindly contribution. It is far from difficult to understand the story as we have it so far, and crucial that we recognize that these first three travelers are quite similar to ourselves. We know both sides.

We can become distracted, often inappropriately, by the roles attached to those who, following the beaten man, precede us along this road. They should stop because of their positions and responsibilities, their upbringing and heritage, we often hear or say. That may be so, and it is at least part of what is implicit in their being professionally identified. But Jesus does not dwell on what they do not do, and his silence may make our indignant chatter about and suggestions for these two still-mobile journeyers recoil noisily on ourselves. All he narrates is that they pass by, with all of their good and bad reasons to which we can so easily relate, on the other side. The victim remains alone. The first two who might stop are, perhaps like us, good people, busy people with legitimate and conflicting calls on their livelihoods. But wherever they are headed, they go on their way seeing little but enough, safer going on than stopping, uncommitted to the man, untouched by him, unasked for anything by him as well. The parable seems to make no mark on them. We may wonder what they are thinking as they hurry past on the other side, and I, at least, can fill it in. I, journeying busily on, would be—am—engaging in the debate of self-justification and winning it. My reasons for hugging my side of the road, eyes averted now, are increasingly compelling to me as I review, rehearse, and recite them.

Our minds filled with both seeing and avoiding the supine figure of Jesus' story, we turn to the psalm, this time not to its beginning but to its crisis point;[3] the speaker, also prone, catches our attention:

> 6 Enemies predict the worst fate for me:
>   "How soon till this one dies,
>   how soon forgotten?"
> 7 Visitors all wish me well
>   but they come seeking bad news
>   to gossip on the street.
> 8 My enemies whisper, and spread the worst about me:
> 9 "Something fatal has taken hold,
>   this one will not get well."
> 10 Even my trusted friend
>   who used to eat with me,
>   now turns on me (Ps 41:6-10).

The psalmist catches up quickly with the beaten man we left breathing with difficulty at the side of the Jericho road. Though our robbed man may be unconscious, he need not be. And the words of this psalmist fit as well in his mouth as they do in the vague present context of the psalm. Psalm parts are readily interchangeable, conveniently packaged for a trip. Overt foes whom the suffering psalmist quotes here are clear in their phrasings, hoping that the recovery will fail to take hold. Their malicious words ring out boldly. Friends are little better, gathering around the sickbed and peering at the chart, struggling to bring sympathetic frowns to their faces but scarcely able to restrain their delight. The questions of the foes—"How long can she last?" or "She'll never be able to shake that condition off!"—are virtually indistinguishable from the murmurs of friends who tell the worst to those not able to come to get their own good news. The psalmist offers in this scene dialogue for the story Jesus has begun in our parable, and so far this person in distress finds the enemies and the friends, the robbers and the clerical passersby, virtually indistinguishable.[4] There are two sides and most of the traffic is on the other side. Hovering over the bedside, these visitors are nonetheless clearly on the other side. The infirm, perhaps well able to cope in the midst of health, is shocked to discover a new position. How different we look to ourselves lying down in weakness rather than bending solicitously over others in our own good health.

We can see, perhaps more clearly in this text than in the other, that the other side is not simply a matter of the physical, crucial and diagnostic though that is. That some of those involved with the psalmist are former friends posing still behind a veneer of friendship, pretending to something that fools only themselves, intensifies the pain that this bedridden individual feels. One in particular has risen from the table of fellowship to wish a host and friend ill. To rephrase the psalm plaint for the lips of Luke's Jerusalem visitor: those who performed my offering with me in Jerusalem have failed to help me out of danger. The prior bond makes the present betrayal worse, as does the hypocrisy, the self-deception that continues to work for the psalmist's friends as it distances her. Whether these enemies are the perpetrators of the sick person's condition seems moot. Their fake concern is overridden by their audible whispers. At a moment of vulnerability they go off to do their talking of one who is not able to speak up for herself. Why should they help? There may be more in it for them to stand by, lurking at the edge. In this recital the victim and the muggers may be longtime friends, appearances to the contrary notwithstanding.

So as we return to the parable and to the latest passerby we have a clear sense of what is deficient, what required. Jesus continues,

> "But a Samaritan while traveling came near him; and when he saw him, he was moved with pity. He went to him and bandaged his wounds, having poured oil and wine on them. Then he put him on his own animal,

brought him to an inn, and took care of him. The next day he took out two denarii, gave them to the innkeeper, and said, 'Take care of him; and when I come back, I will repay you whatever more you spend'" (Luke 10:33-35).

As is long familiar to us, the gentilic this journeyer bears is immediately suspect and opposite to that of the priest and Levite. The Samaritan is not even a bona fide Gentile but more a renegade Jew, looked at from at least one perspective.[5] He is not poor, as we can easily see since he is traveling with at the very least plenty for his own needs; perhaps he is a merchant of some sort or the servant of a wealthy master. He is not the evangelist's first story character to unload some of his stuff rather than store it for a later time; the Samaritan shares oil and wine, property, ego, even risks his safety and health. And like the others who precede him, ourselves included, he has his own excellent reasons for passing by on the other side: danger, conflicting responsibilities, understandable fears, past experience, family awaiting him at home. Rehearsing these excuses or disincentives again reminds us of their validity. They are similar to those we envision for the priest and Levite and surely for ourselves. These reasons for not stopping are authentic. If they are not—or insofar as we try to palm off fake excuses—we can easily be talked out of them. The parable's strength depends on the truthfulness of the scenario. The other side is indeed dangerous for all of us.

What makes the third journeyer different from the first two, however, is that when he like the others sees the man, the Samaritan is filled with compassion. To be filled with compassion is not a choice, a deed, or an entitlement. It is, at the moment it floods in, not controllable, though we can perhaps manage to keep it at bay if we are vigilant in our life choices. The Samaritan may be caught off guard by his compassion. It is arguably easier and more convenient for him to avoid its welling up. The point, I think, is not to romanticize this man into being thrilled to help; if we find ourselves reluctant or unwilling we ought not to give in to the temptation of making it too easy for him. But once he sees the needy one at the roadside, as he begins to look more closely, his heart goes out to the man and is drawn down to the injured man's side of the road, which at once becomes his own. He takes his own goods, or in any case those for which he is responsible, and spends them on the injured man as though he were a beloved or a self—which indeed he becomes once the mercy of the Samaritan encircles him. His compassion impels him to the other side of the road, prompts him to the spending of his livelihood; lacking the compassion, the others are able to hurry on by, their goods intact.

We may be of the mind that the Samaritan becomes more involved than he needs to. He administers first aid on site, next helps the man to a safe place and tends him additionally, finally leaves the equivalent of a blank check or a generously-backed credit card with the innkeeper. It might suffice, and would not be bad, comparatively speaking, to simply hurry on and dial 911. The outsider's lavish and expensive procedures are dangerous; imagine unpacking valuable supplies at the scene of a robbery! Bringing the wounded man to the inn is equally hazardous to the Samaritan whose safety is hardly enhanced in the company of a wounded man, a man from the other side doing a favor for one of "us."[6] Jesus, brilliant storyteller that he is, does not fill in more detail about this man, inviting us perhaps to do it ourselves. Who he is, what he does, what rewards we may grant his generosity—these are not the main point.

And so we move the scene along a bit past the place where it breaks off, to envision various reactions. Like the other parables, this one is not tracked to its logical ending; it may be less patient of romanticizing than we assume. Let us push beyond the story line we have though still holding on to the scenario as our metaphor has shaped it so far. First we can identify with the suspicion of the innkeeper who knows a scam when she sees one: a Samaritan dumping a near-corpse, perhaps having secreted for later retrieval all of the beaten man's possessions, leaving a fraction of what was in the purse, promising to stop in later. It sounds just like the shady shenanigans to be expected from that type, from the other side, with their ways. Or perhaps as the beaten man regains his consciousness and sees the Samaritan leaning over his bruised body he signals—verbally or by instinctive gesture—the same fearful suspicion. The injured man may not be so grateful to the Samaritan; he may be considerably displeased at the temerity of the man who dares to cross from the other side and become so involved. The Samaritan may well understand such an unguarded revulsion but it has to be a painful action to witness, perhaps—if he is fortunate—a humbling moment for the robbed man to remember, should his initial reaction have proved unfounded. Such reactions may be irrational but they are not unimaginable, if we are honest. At our moments of humiliation having our side of the road to ourselves is the least we can expect, surely what we deserve, we insist.

Harper Lee's classic novel (and film), *To Kill a Mockingbird*, set in the South during the 1930s, explores among its other subplots the story of Tom Robinson, a black man who gives his life—and whose life is taken—because he says that he feels sorry for and presumes to assist a poor white girl. She, having invited him to do so for complex and undiscerned reasons of her own, turns in horror from and denial at her own deed, once its character becomes clearer, and accuses him of rape. The black man's capacity to see the poor white girl, lawyer Atticus Finch's courage to cross over to Tom's side of the road, the Finch children's journey to the viewpoint of the mysterious and frightening Boo Radley all show the same concern at work. It is no small thing for a Samaritan to cross to our side of the road but it may look to us an outrage, and though we may need him to do so, we repudiate him for the deed. Such reactions from us leave the Samaritan in a terrible quandary of his own. Once we can see that he in many ways has little to gain and much to lose by crossing to the other side and letting his compassion involve him in a good deed that becomes an accusation, he has to decide what to do. His anger, his hurt, the injustice of it, the danger may well drive him back to his own side of the road, shaking off the dust as a witness against those who refuse his compassion though they benefit from it. The Samaritan may end up paying heavily for what his compassion impels him to do.

We return to our psalm hoping that the psalmist, lying in distress, has found a benefactor. She seems to hope so as well, seems to count on it as the prayer starts out:

> 2 Blest are those ready to help the poor.
>   In hard times God repays their care.
> 3 God watches, protects,
>   blesses them in their land;
>   let no enemy swallow them up!
> 4 God comforts them on their sick bed
>   and nurses them to health (Ps 41:2-4).

A few moments ago the psalm might have sounded a bit different in our ears. We can imagine the Samaritan, ready indeed to help, murmuring it as he rushes over to the side of the injured citizen, praying to God for strength to do what he sees as his responsibility. God, far from abandoning the poor and the sick as they endure their trials, sends someone to assist: if not a priest or Levite, at the very least or very most a compassionate Samaritan. It is the sort of confidence we read in the persistence of the widow in Luke 18. Those with a special and traditional claim on God can with confidence press their need forward. Though the sick psalmist is surrounded by friends and thugs—can hardly tell one from the other—still she awaits the one who will comfort and nurse her back to health. But now, having crossed to consider the scene with a suspicious innkeeper, with the resentful robbed man, and with the humiliated and angered Samaritan, we may wonder. Where is God's repayment in all of this?

> 5 I said, "God pity me,
>   heal me for I have failed you."

Who is the speaker of the psalm, of these lines of lament? Whose voice is begging forgiveness? What failure is the speaker confessing? The uncertain context of the psalm makes it difficult to know. From where in the sickroom is the voice arising? From which side of the road? It may be the genuine contrition of those who pass by on the other side or of those in the psalm who hasten out to plan the funeral of the person who is not quite dead. It can easily be the priest and the Levite who, like ourselves, may sincerely wish they might do better—and who with enough help may indeed do so.

> 11 Pity me, God, restore me
>   so I can pay them back.
> 12 Then I will know you favor me
>   when my foes cannot prevail.
> 13 I am innocent; uphold me! (Ps 41:5, 11-13).

Or is this cry for compassion rising from Luke's beaten traveler, regretting his obvious reaction to his rescuer, praying to turn his wrath rather to those who are his real opponents once he understands better the chain of events that so interrupt his journey? Is it perhaps the Samaritan himself begging the compassion of God on his own anger and the strength of God for his own repaying? Is it the psalmist wishing she were not so adept at cataloguing the words and faces she registers? Who is on the side that needs healing, and who on the side to offer it? What is our response in the presence of the prayer for retaliation? If prayer is announcement of our own justification this plea is certainly embarrassingly out of place. But if prayer is our honest blurtings to God, then it is a mirror for us. If we spend most of our emotional time and empathy trailing along behind the priest and the Levite—sheepish though we sometimes are to be caught on their side of the road—then the nakedness of this plea to get even need not outrage us too much. Once we choose sides and decide we have to stick with our own, the desire for revenge is simply a point farther along the spectrum from the others, an additional polite wall between them and us. Insofar as we settle safely on our side we may not yet understand the circuitry constantly linking anger and compassion, the alchemy turning one into the other. Our reactions may give us a valuable clue: to what extent can we understand the anger of the vulnerable man whose rescue depends on someone he can feel little grateful to? the rage of the Samaritan, falsely suspected, feeling little satisfaction from a deed that only increases his low esteem in the eyes of those who see it? the grief of the psalmist who has let down her own companions, whatever they may have done to deserve it? If we do not recognize yet their prayer for revenge perhaps we may need to spend more time in their company.

In Jesus' story the one who finally assists is not different just because he is an outsider. In itself that is not enough. The Samaritan is different because what prompts him is compassion. As we have seen elsewhere in these biblical texts compassion is not something we control or manage; it directs us. The most we can do is live in such a way that we allow mercy some exercise, still feel its flow through our systems on occasion, even as often as possible. Though we cannot commandeer compassion we can restrict it from our lives if we wish to make that choice. There are plenty of voices to advise us that it is in our interests to do so. The priest and the Levite can mount a good case for their actions, perhaps a more satisfied one than the Samaritan can manage to offer for his deed.

But Jesus, speaking and acting, is not willing to let it rest there. Breaking off the journey tale, he addresses those listening with a question and a blessing. He asks: "Which of these three, do you think, was a neighbor to the man who fell into the hands of the robbers?" Far from the original perspective of the lawyer's own point of view in asking both "what must I do" and "who is my neighbor," Jesus helps him lie at the edge of the road and ponder something a little different: who acts as neighbor, who "comforts us on our sickbed and nurses us to health" (Ps 41:4)? The psalmist identifies the only nurse on the scene as God; Jesus clothes the suspect in an outsider uniform. The lawyer, avoiding for whatever reasons the titles of the roles strikes the heart of it: the one who shows compassion. It is, of course, a correct answer as we can see from both the psalm's pleas to God for compassion and the parable's identification of the man so moved. The neighbor is the one compassion sends to the other side, whatever may befall him or her upon arriving.

Jesus now finishes the discussion by agreeing and commissioning: "Go and do likewise" (Luke 10:36-37). "Likewise" is not a thing one does to inherit something else, it hardly need be said by now. It is an adverb, not a noun. To act habitually in such a way, impelled by compassion at one moment to this side of the road and now again to the other is confusing, disorienting, anger-producing. We may feel insufficiently comfortable where our compassion directs us. We may even lose the sense of which is our side and which the other.

Compassion is not a hothouse plant, delicate and best saved in isolation. Compassion itself is a gift, accepted and nurtured, exercised and consequently bedraggled. It need not—will not—always feel good to the compassionate, though we may scarcely notice such a thing on our way down the road if that is where we need to head for the moment. But we may hope that someone is praying for us as well, mixing in with their other designs on us the plea for pity on us, a gift that can bring us over to the side we never thought to be on.

Book 1 of the psalter thus ends with a doxology:

> 14 Blessed be the Lord,
>   God of Israel for ever.
>   Amen! Amen! (Ps 41:14).

NOTES: CHAPTER 9

[1] At Mark 12:29-31 and Matt 22:37-40 Jesus himself offers this blend, which we can note is from Deuteronomy 6:4-5 and Leviticus 19:17-18. There is nothing wrong with the answer.

[2] Bruce Malina and Richard L. Rohrbaugh, *A Social Science Commentary on the Synoptic Gospels* (Minneapolis: Fortress, 1992) 41–42.

[3] Carroll Stuhlmueller's commentary, *Psalms 1* (Wilmington: Michael Glazier, 1983) 222, shows a structure for this psalm, its compact and chiastic architecture part of its communication as we saw with Psalm 8. Though such a feature can be valuable to explore, it is also legitimate to overlook it for the moment. If we are to become at home in the biblical texts we need to feel free to examine them in a variety of ways.

[4] Toni Craven's study, *The Book of Psalms* (Collegeville: Michael Glazier, 1992) demonstrates a number of ways to interlink the psalms. Though she, like most others who write on them, helps us to understand the forms or conventions that give a few, standard shapes to the short prayers, she spends even more time assisting us to unpack the many ways in which the psalms rise from human experience and hence are familiar to us.

[5]James D. Newsome, *Greeks, Romans, Jews: Currents of Culture and Belief in the New Testament World* (Philadelphia: Trinity Press International, 1992) 122–127, helps us understand the probable mind-set of the reference. Samaritans, living in the region that was once the heartland of monarchic Israel, are clearly not pictured as Jews and yet it is clear to historians that they shared many of the traditions of Galilean and Judean groups. They are pictured as the classic "other side," made to seem deviant when what is more likely is that they are one of a number of communities within an Israelite tradition.

[6]Kenneth E. Bailey, *Through Peasant Eyes* 52, likens the Samaritan approaching the inn with a beaten man in tow to a Plains Indian bringing a scalped cowboy for help to a frontier town. Appearances are open to tragic misunderstanding.

10

Conclusion

*H*aving now walked with and through eight metaphors and their textual settings, let us consider once again what it is we have done and reflect a little more panoramically upon how it has worked. If we were to choose a fresh metaphor to help us explore the process of reading these figures in psalm and parable texts, it might be the journey. "The psalms bring us home to God, no matter how we are dressed, how we feel, what we have done or left undone," Carroll Stuhlmueller reminds us.[1] The journey is the life of the pilgrim, the paths of human existence we choose and are given to travel during our span of days. Luke has set these distinctive parables on the journey to Jerusalem Jesus makes with his companions and the various other people they encounter "on the way." Attentive readers of the Lukan chapters will notice that the travel motif and context is not particularly developed by the evangelist; at Luke 17:11 they seem to have made little geographical progress since Luke 9:52! The travel narrative serves not to review Palestinian geography but to show us something else about trips, and the challenge of the metaphors is to move us as well, from one stage of awareness and response to another, paradoxically to root us more deeply. So the figure of the journey helps us understand where we have come from and to glimpse the road ahead—and to settle in.

As we well know, travel is not simply a matter of starting at home and arriving efficiently at some desired destination. We may not be eager to leave home or to go anywhere other than where we already comfortably are. We may rather have a vague desire to go somewhere, to leave where we are, but, uncertain about our arrival point, we hesitate about various facets of the matter: what route to select, with whom to go, what to take, how much time to leave are all questions we weigh, choices we revise many times. Nor is it simply a matter of booking tickets on the Concorde and then napping until the captain turns the "fasten seat belt" sign back on and bids the flight personnel to prepare for landing. The travel process of going is itself a major part of our experience even if we expect to be more suitably focused on the excitement of departure or the relief of eventual arrival. A journey almost by definition is fresh, adventure-prone, somewhat outside our control. Things happen to us as we travel that are unlikely to befall us at home. We change en route, perhaps imperceptibly, sometimes more dramatically. Offering self-knowledge, the journey can draw us through transformation as well as provide transportation.

The most labored journey I recall making was "The Tortilla Marathon," a ten-day walk from Santa Barbara to the town of Tijuana just across the Mexico-California border. The distance was 250 miles, the purpose to raise money for orphanages and other work with the poor that went on in Tijuana; the walkers were mostly students and a few teachers who had spent weekends helping in Tijuana and were eager to assist in securing some financial resources for the projects there. Our preparations were extensive: long practice walks to insure (or make likely) that we could all cope with twenty-five miles a day for ten days in a row, solicitations of funds from sponsors who could learn about the project they were supporting, concern about how little or how much to wear and carry. The organizers of the walk planned the route, lined up food and accommodations and all other services we would require along the way. Such amenities, though inevitably simple, were crucial.

What I experienced en route, however, was another whole world, not detached from the rigorous walk to raise money and awareness about the plight of the poor a few miles south of San Diego but mysteriously intermixed with that part of the project. I found it quickly became boring to walk several hours a day in the company of the same people once the superficialities of conversation were exhausted. It was, in fact, exhausting to have to keep beginning to tell of one's self for ten days in a row to various of the two hundred or so participants. I had just completed my doctorate, a labor of a number of years. That seemed to me an impressive piece of information to share about who I was, but not everyone was all that responsive or congratulatory. Others, in fact, had irritating facets of themselves that they brought to the conversation all too frequently; the peripatetic group became a sort of captive community for those who had problems to process day after day. The walking, even in the warm June sun, was not so difficult for me as were the evenings, filled with group activities reminiscent of summer camp since most of the walkers were teenagers. A few of the older walkers became oddly willing to walk a few more miles at the end of a day in order to share an ice cream cone with an intimate circle and avoid whatever was on the group schedule.

There was a couple, somewhat peripherally involved with the walking, who accompanied us in a recreational vehicle to help carry part of the gear. In their trailer was not only a shower stall for one—vastly preferable to some of the other bathing options—but a little refrigerator replenished frequently with a jug of inexpensive white wine. The idea of taking an evening shower in the trailer after the day's twenty-five miles rather than in a gym with a cast of thousands became an obsession with me, though I tried each morning (clean) to argue myself out of needing to do something different from most of the other journeyers. But I had several showers in the trailer, and a few glasses of wine as the days wore on. I found myself getting tired of being proselytized about the poor, hearing about the social justice work of those who had organized the walk and had been doing so for the past ten years or so. I became grumpy about the egos (of various ages) who grabbed the spotlight in whatever way they could, people from whom I could not get away. The trip was a valuable one, but for many reasons beyond the simple accomplishment of it. Raising money was great, important for the Tijuana projects; performing a demanding physical feat was gratifying. But I learned a lot about myself in ten days that I had not known before, though the traits I discovered were hardly fresh. The insights I had were not bad: pining for some silence, feeling the urge to manufacture a false life history so I could flaunt some new data just for a change of tape, feeling obliged to waste some uncongenial insincere bonhomie to repay a few hot showers and cold glasses of Chablis were points of access to deeper possibilities. The journey took me to many new places besides the coast highway of Southern California. The walking taught me a lot about rootedness.

Why is the process of reading psalms and parables through metaphor able to be considered through the screen of the journey? Jesus, walking along with friends, prays; Luke notes it (10:21-22, 11:1-4). Plausibly, as a Jew, he prays the psalms; and thus rooted he generates the parables. The psalms are one version of the journey of Israel: not only the historical itinerary but a cross-section of the projects of God in which the Jewish people participate. The 150 prayers that we have explore a terrain beloved of God, not only the geography that is specified but the many facets of nature that also comprise the poems. In addition to being the journey of the whole people, the psalms with their vast diversity are the prayers of individuals. They show us every mood, offer us every human feeling, lead us in and out of many specific situations. They speak right out bluntly about our tremendous capacities for good and for evil. They demolish our false stage sets,[2] leaving us a bit more exposed and unsupported by props than we had planned to be. We may on occasion feel a bit outraged at them, a little or a lot holier than they are; we shrink from harboring some of their sentiments. But for the most part those postures are denied to those who pray psalms continually in all our moods, in the ups and downs of our life, in good times and in hard times. There is not a lot in the psalms that is unthinkable or unsayable, so far as I can see—little that is undoable. The psalms free us to see ourselves as we are, to see that we are like others, that we have plenty to learn from nature, to recall that we are beloved by God as well as in trouble on occasion. The psalms free us to talk about everything with God and with each other—with our friends and certainly with our opponents. The psalms remove nothing from the agenda of humanization, cross nothing off the itinerary of our pilgrimage.

The gospel travel narrative, filled with episodes and parables, is not radically different although more compressed. It rolls out under our feet Jesus' teaching in context as he copes with issues and questions people bring to him or he to them, offering insight as to how things are in the kingdom of God, which is another way of describing the realm where God's favorite projects are going along well. But the parables are also Jesus articulating for himself the implications of what he is being asked to do, his own bringing to fuller understanding the way in which he is collaborating with God on those same projects. Jesus gives out a lot as he goes, and presumably he receives a lot as he journeys too, though there is less detail about it. There is every reason to assume that Jesus factors into the parables his prayer, his experience with God, his concern about what lies ahead; the parables express these depths as well as his keen observations of the natural world and social culture through which they are all walking on the way to their destination. Jesus tells and shows us, experiences for himself as well as offering to us what it is to be on pilgrimage with friend and foe, sustained by God, surrounded by nature, coping with life circumstances. Those, after all, are the subjects of the psalms and the parables: trees, sheep and shepherds, sides of the road, stored up goods, feelings of entitlement, concerns about status. Before asking a final time just how the metaphors work for us, let us review what they disclosed to us.

The planted tree, at first looking too static for our needs, actually offered us a model of intense activity. We came to consider its challenge for us to be not only deeply generative but to be responsive as well to the hands of the gardener and the care offered to us. Receptivity is part of our rootedness. When we considered our stature and status we quickly felt disoriented, since there was no fixed place from which we could do our measuring. Depending where we were standing—under the stars, above creeping creatures, crowned regent by God or perhaps reporting on the quality of our stewardship—we felt tall and small by turns. We saw a powerful figure give of his livelihood not once but repeatedly to others and not shrink but increase in stature in our eyes; his sons, not minding to belittle him in order to enlarge themselves, offered me, at least, a pair of measures and balances familiar to my mode of operating. Searching several faces that were themselves seeking security, we recognized reflections of our own quest. Security is not an acquisition on which we can count, even if we seek it appropriately as did the psalmist, following her heart to God's face; the self-satisfied man at prayer whose security seemed coextensive with his own efforts and the self-emptying one who begged mercy from God may have looked more different to us than they did to Luke's widow, about to make a generous gift of her security with her last coins.

In the figures of entitlement and moral ecology we looked more systemically at our behaviors. What may have seemed a relationship of *quid pro quo* between God and the psalmist or the widow and the judge gave way to petitions on the basis of a shared past. That the ones asking have developed a long-term relationship with the ones petitioned incessantly provides the hope and expectation of a response, even the likelihood of it. But especially if we consider the possibility that the widow is the deity and the judge the curmudgeonly human being we know that begging does not force an answer. The quality of the relationship is what is key. A similar insight unfolded from considering our actions not so much as discrete deeds to be weighed and condemned by a stern judge or effectively remediated by a divine paramedic; rather they are assessable as patterns of responsible living in our moral environment. How we make our choices in relationality with other beings, how we respond to the choices of others that affect us becomes more a matter of the long haul than messes to be coped with at once. Such metaphors do not remove the divine judge and healer but make us more responsible for the general health of those with whom we share the environment; a newly shaped attitude will radically convert our relationship with the judge and healer and surely with the environment.

When we looked at the shepherd and the sheep we were immediately brought into a cycle of reciprocity and interdependence. The sheep exist for the shepherd who lives for them as well. The vulnerability as well as service became mutual, the roles strangely changeable, the weakness and strength paradoxically intertwined. The stuffed storehouse sounded initially like something to avoid, but what the image disclosed rather to us was the inevitability of our accumulating. The question then was not so much whether to do it but what to save. Our stored goods actually fill us up, enclose us. With some kinds of goods it becomes very difficult to move along the pathway; with other sorts of goods it is much easier to maneuver efficiently. Finally our journey with these texts brought us to a choice of sides: the one that was easier and more natural—and safer—for us or the other side where we would rather not go too often. To have the courage to cross over is not easy, nor is the experience of so doing necessarily rewarded. We may be angry at those who cross onto our side and then angry at ourselves for being so guarded.

The metaphors rely in each case on our common experience, on the accumulation of wisdom each of us has from the human journey. Our familiarity with the symbol of tree or sheep, faces or storehouses helps us understand what the psalms and parables are talking about. We have been there; we dwell there now. But just as intrinsic to the engineering of the metaphor is the element of surprise. The very familiarity of the scenarios invites us to move along with our texts, but then suddenly and skillfully we are offered something unexpected, not foreseen by us for all our cleverness and erudition.

The psalm imagery achieves its surprise partly by exaggeration, by outrageous assertion, by multiplicity of succeeding images. The psalms are like an unruly crowd accompanying us on our journey in a noisy welter, thrusting at us many things that we have the opportunity to consider as we go. We cannot take it all in at once, but what seems irrelevant or obscure at one moment can be stored for reconsideration at a later time. The psalms are not fragile, not needing much to be protected from our rough or fearful handling of them. To leave them neglected on the shelf is more risky than to use them. Matthew Kelty counsels us to go ahead and keep saying them even if in some cases they don't now or don't yet fit. In time our hearts and minds will catch up.[3] The psalms are also able to disconcert and surprise us because they are full of gaps and unexplained shifts for us to cross into, the landing uncertain.

The parables accomplish their goal in a slightly different way, hence contributing to the effective architecture of the metaphors on which they collaborate with their psalmic partners. We feel safe with the parables as Jesus tells them in the gospels, partly because they are so familiar. We sense that we have them figured out and can go at once, at the opening words, to stand with the most virtuous among their narrated characters. But the master-parabler still manages suddenly to surprise us, to catch us off guard; the parable can nip us in an exposed ankle just as we are stepping up to take our place among the good. All of a sudden there is a shift of perspective, a repositioning of the subject or some nuance of it, and we are confronted with a sight—or insight—we had not expected to see. As our life experience expands we hear new things in these old images. Unlike the psalms, which tend to rewind by the end and show us things back under control, the parables break off. What happens next is up to us to finish. These are sophisticated mechanics.

We may also now be in a position to observe some common features of our metaphors, a set of characteristics that did not emerge when we considered them one at a time. All of them envision and utilize mobility. None is static, certainly not the planted tree or even the storehouse, or our status, or some presumption about entitlement. In every case there is motion and change involved—a journey. The metaphors, with their psalmic and parabolic particulars, show us a menu of moves we might make. Similarly, all of them are relational. In some instances we can see it at once: the searching faces, the shepherd and sheep, the crossings to the other side. But we discover the tree also to be extensively relational. The metaphor involving the warrior and the king and the widow and the judge is not a matter of labeling roles and identifying jobs but of watching the intricacy of bonds that enclose and intertwine helpers and helped.

As we consider the functions of the metaphors as well as their content, and as we reflect on their challenges to us to move in the midst of many complex relationships, we finally arrive at the question of how we can choose well even if we have been given some new insight. It is not always enough simply to know. Why will we be able to accept and participate in the transformation journey that these figures offer to take us on? A few possibilities can be suggested. Jesus, journeying with those he loves and toward those he loves, speaks persistently about our need to move out from our isolation, our narrow skins, our self-important and smug auto-estimations. He challenges us with the fruitless tree helped by the gardener, the selfish farmer called by God to make an accounting of his life, the fired manager looking for allies, the judge allowing the persistence of the widow to jog his stubbornness. More positively he shows us the father who rushes out to tell and show both sons of his love, the shepherd who gives a life for the sheep, a sinner throwing himself on the mercy of God, a Samaritan who is rushed by his compassion—not by his common sense or self-interest—to the other side of the road.

This mercy or compassion, sometimes named, often shown, occasionally prominently absent, is what moves and binds all of these elements in relationship. Compassion is not simply a warm feeling. It is closer to wearied weeping or to churning discomfort or to a sense of losing control. In each metaphor we have considered the crucial insight and invitation is to redraw the boundaries of ourselves, not perfectly perhaps, but a little bigger, ever more inclusively. It is not something we will be able to decide on and then complete handily. It is too difficult for that; our self-motivation will break down soon. Compassion, such as the tax collector begs from God and the prodigal father and the generous Samaritan exhibit, is received as a beneficence, comes as a response, an almost undeniable movement to enclose another in some way. It arises from the recognition that the other is not really so different from myself, that what I disdain in her is undoubtedly resident in me as well, probably quite prominently. It is an ultimate—if not always thrilled—willingness to share my goods, my energies, my livelihood and life with those who present themselves.

Why should Jesus be talking with us about this matter as he journeys toward Jerusalem? The advice is perennial of course, and one cannot hear too much of it. But his encounters and ruminations supply the very energy that sustains him as he prays the psalms of his people and articulates the parables, draws him to the city where he dies like a mother hen unable to gather her chicks under her wings no matter the desire and the effort. Jesus journeys toward the particular project of God that is his to do by articulating and embodying compassion. The reigning of God comes closer and fuller as Jesus brings it into experience, as his hands and feet, eyes and mouth make its features clearer to those attentive. If the metaphors in the psalms and parables have shown us some new things about ourselves and each other—and about God and creation—and have surprised and challenged us into insights about the journey ahead, then we perhaps need to be spending some time as he did: divesting ourselves of what we can let go of, offering what others might need, abandoning insofar as we can the struggle to buttress our status and achievements, to defend and insist on our entitlements, to measure our importance with the special ruler that we so painstakingly designed for the task. We need not think we are magnanimously and generously giving something up, self-righteously donating our invaluable achievements to the careless voraciousness of others. Compassion offers us far more than we have guarded on our own, can draw us compellingly into the intimacy of new relationships with God and all of God's friends.

We recall the importance of knowing the destination if good choices are to be made about the trip. The goal for Jesus and those with him is not really just Jerusalem itself but rather what that city symbolizes: the presence of and a key access to God. We are not so much struggling toward a destination as being gently and firmly guided there in company with many others who will help us by their own gifts and neediness as we assist them by our own strengths and weaknesses. Compassion is a welling response to something that has become undeniable to us. Born of insight, nurtured in prayer that becomes more ready to acknowledge neediness and interdependence, the sort of expansion of our borders that is envisioned in these figures needs practice and will thrive when exercised. While we are practicing compassion—in whatever size comes to hand, from the two-coin size the widow shows in Luke 21:1-4 to the larger contribution Zacchaeus makes in 19:1-10 to the giant economy deed contributed by Jesus himself in chapters 22–23—we can be bringing our struggles and joys to prayer, discussing them with other pilgrims. We will find, at least a good deal of the time, our efforts shared by others with whom we unpack our own, our burdens carried by those who happen to be going our way for a while. We will find ourselves attended to, restored when we are feeling dried up, regenerated by the love of others, nurtured like a tree planted . . . .

NOTES: CHAPTER 10

[1]"The Book of Psalms," concluding essay to accompany *The Psalter* (Chicago: Liturgy Training Publications, 1995) xxi.

[2]Matthew Kelty, "The Psalms as Prayer," 84–85.

[3]Kelty, "The Psalms as Prayer," 86.

Bibliography

Bailey, Kenneth E. *Poet and Peasant* and *Through Peasant Eyes: A Literary-Critical Approach to the Parables of Luke.* Combined volume. Grand Rapids: Eerdmans, 1976, 1980.

Barton, Stephen. *The Spirituality of the Gospels.* Peabody, Mass.: Hendrickson, 1992.

Berry, Wendell. *Sex, Economy, Freedom and Community.* New York: Pantheon, 1992.

Caird, G. B. *The Language and Imagery of the Bible.* London: Duckworth, 1980.

Craven, Toni. *The Book of Psalms.* Collegeville: Michael Glazier, 1992.

Darr, John. *On Character Building: The Reader and the Rhetoric of Characterization in Luke-Acts.* Louisville: Westminster/John Knox, 1992.

Donahue, John R., S.J. *The Gospel in Parable: Metaphor, Narrative, and Theology in the Synoptic Gospels.* Philadelphia: Fortress, 1988.

Dornisch, Loretta. *A Woman Reads the Gospel of Luke.* Collegeville: The Liturgical Press, 1996.

Fitzmyer, Joseph A. *The Gospel according to Luke X–XXIV. Introduction, Translation, Notes.* Garden City, N.Y.: Doubleday, 1983.

Kelty, Matthew, O.C.S.O. *Sermons in a Monastery: Chapter Talks.* Kalamazoo: Cistercian Publications, 1983.

McKenna, Megan. *Parables. The Arrows of God.* Maryknoll, N.Y.: Orbis, 1994.

Macky, Peter W. *The Centrality of Metaphor to Biblical Thought: A Method for Interpretation of the Bible.* Lewiston, N.Y.: Edwin Mellen Biblical Press, 1990.

Malina, Bruce, and Richard L. Rohrbaugh. *A Social Science Commentary on the Synoptic Gospels.* Minneapolis: Fortress, 1992.

Mandela, Nelson. *Long Walk to Freedom: The Autobiography of Nelson Mandela.* Boston: Little, Brown & Co., 1994.

McFague, Sallie. *Metaphorical Theology: Models of God in Religious Language.* Philadelphia: Fortress, 1982.

Miller, Patrick D., Jr. *Interpreting the Psalms.* Philadelphia: Fortress, 1986.

Newsome, James D. *Greeks, Romans, Jews: Currents of Culture and Belief in the New Testament World*. Philadelphia: Trinity Press International, 1992.

Ricoeur, Paul. *The Rule of Metaphor: Multi-disciplinary Studies of the Creation of Meaning in Language*. London: Routledge and Kegan Paul, 1978.

Ryken, Leland. "Metaphor in the Psalms." *Christianity and Literature* 31 (1982) 9–30.

Sanders, E. P. *The Historical Figure of Jesus*. London: Allen Lane, Penguin Press, 1993.

Saldarini, Anthony. *Pharisees, Scribes and Sadducees in Palestinian Society: A Sociological Approach*. Wilmington: Michael Glazier, 1988.

Stuhlmueller, Carroll. *Psalms 1*. Wilmington: Michael Glazier, 1983.

Trible, Phyllis. *Rhetorical Criticism: Context, Method, and the Book of Jonah*. Minneapolis: Fortress, 1994.

Whiston, William, trans. *The Works of Josephus*. Peabody, Mass.: Hendrickson, 1987.